Annette Funicello
America's Sweetheart

An Unauthorized Biography
By Marc Shapiro

Copyright © 2013 by Marc Shapiro

Riverdale Avenue Books
5676 Riverdale Avenue, Suite 101
Riverdale, NY 10471

All rights reserved. No part of this book may be reproduced or transmitted in any form or by any means, electronic or mechanical, including photocopying, without permission in writing from the publisher.

Printed in the United States of America.

First Edition May 2013

Cover by Scott Carpenter
Cover photo: Globe-Photos
Formatting by www.formatting4U.com

ISBN: electronic 978-1-62601-033-8
ISBN: print 978-1-62601-034-5

www.riverdaleavebooks.com

To my wife, Nancy…my fantasy come to life. My daughter Rachael. Granddaughter Lily. Ian (DFIU). Mike, Brady, Fitch. All the good humans and animals. Lori…as always number one in my book. Louise. Riverdale Avenue Books. As always the good books, the good music, and the good art. It's there if you look hard enough. Karma, do unto others and everything in your head and heart that gets you through the day. And finally to the memory of Annette. They don't make lives like yours anymore. More's the pity.

TABLE OF CONTENTS

ACKNOWLEDGMENTS	*i*
AUTHOR'S NOTE: This Is Where Things Get Interesting	*iii*
INTRODUCTION...Our Royalty	1
ONE...Coping In 1995	4
TWO...The Road to California	12
THREE...I Can't Sing ...You're Hired	28
FOUR...The Wonder Year	33
FIVE...Front and Center	47
SIX...Now It's Time to Say Goodbye	54
SEVEN...Tall Paul	60
EIGHT...Reality Check	74
NINE...Hit the Beach	92
TEN...Love and Marriage	104
ELEVEN...Through Sickness and In Health	115
TWELVE...Alone	118
THIRTEEN...Secrets	124
FOURTEEN...The Big Reveal	132
FIFTEEN...Search for a Cure	136
SIXTEEN...The Good Fight	141
SEVENTEEN...A Miracle Cure?	145
EPILOGUE...Dancing In Heaven	149
FILMOGRAPHY	153
DISCOGRAPHY	157
ABOUT THE AUTHOR	164

ACKNOWLEDGMENTS

As with most biographies, *Annette Funicello: America's Sweetheart* was a book that drew from many sources.

First and foremost a big thank you to Annette's excellent 1994 autobiography, *A Dream Is a Wish Your Heart Makes*, which brought to light many wonderful moments.

I would like to thank Carl Gardner of the group The Coasters, Freddy "Boom Boom" Cannon, Tommy Sands, and Richard Sherman for their time and their memories of Annette.

Sam Arkoff's lively autobiography, *Flying through Hollywood by the Seat of My Pants*, brought entertaining insights into Annette's "Beach Movie" period. Keith Keller's book, *The Mickey Mouse Club Scrapbook* likewise answered many questions regarding Annette's first show business steps. Jerry Bowles' fascinating book, *Forever Hold Your Banner High*, brought to light a lot of the reality behind the fantasy, as did Lonnie Burr's entertaining autobiography *Confessions of an Accidental Mouseketeer*. I would also like to thank Mike Kirby, creator of the website Way Back Attack

(WayBackAttack.com), the authoritative look at all pre 1970s music, for the super comprehensive list of Annette's recording career.

The following newspapers and magazines helped this author down the long and winding trail: *People, Los Angeles Magazine, Interview, Ladies Home Journal, The New York Times, The Santa Monica Evening Outlook, Los Angeles Herald Examiner, The Disney News, Los Angeles Times, Look, Mirror News, Ladies Circle, The National Enquirer, The Bakersfield Californian, The St. Petersburg Times, USA Today, Associated Press, In Style, Animation* and *Northeast Woman*.

And a thank you to the following websites that helped the cause: CNN.com, E Online, CTV News, WT5.com, Variety.com, TMZ.com, D23.com, The Star.com, About.com, Major Smolinski.com, News Journal.com, TCM Biography.com and NewsMaxHealth.com.

AUTHOR'S NOTES

THIS IS WHERE THINGS GET INTERESTING

You want strange and unusual? Well, try this on for size.

I turned in the original draft of the manuscript for *Annette Funicello: America's Sweetheart* in 1997. Legal went over this puppy with the proverbial fine-tooth comb. Editing was done and done. Galley proofs had been issued and, likewise checked to within an inch of their lives. So far so good. Except for one minor detail...

There was not an actual release date.

The publisher in question, who shall remain nameless because I'm not in the habit of throwing people under the bus, had his own agenda when it came to releasing the book. The advance check cleared, so this writer could wait. But the years went by, the book was still nowhere to be found on the publisher's schedule and, most importantly, Annette was still very much alive and, by association, making the manuscript as it stood at that point woefully in need of an update.

So all concerned parties waited and waited.

Flash forward to April 8, 2013. After a 26 year battle with multiple sclerosis (MS), Annette passed away due to complications from her disease. A quick call by my agent discovered that after holding the manuscript for 16 years, the publisher now has no desire to publish it.

Now this is where things get really interesting.

Back in the stone age of publishing (also known as 1997), electronic publishing was just a gleam in the literary community's collective eye. It was such an abstract concept that most publishers had no interest in the "pipe dream" as a way to turn a book into mad profit and, consequently, did not have an e-book clause in their contracts. But when Riverdale Avenue Books jumped into the breach and indicated they would publish the book, the publisher in question had an official letter written that effectively returned all rights to the manuscript, including e-rights, to the author, who immediately passed them on to Riverdale. It all seemed fine until…

That old devil technology delivered a sucker punch.

Nobody had a full copy of the manuscript. Not the original publisher. Not the agent and not the author. Because again things were done differently back in 1997. Manuscripts were still being mailed to agents and publishers. People changed locations. Packing boxes got lost.

Annette Funicello: America's Sweetheart was a phantom that existed but, in that all important completed form, was nowhere to be found. A frantic search of my office and files (a true journey into hell) miraculously produced fragments of the original manuscript. Some completed chapters, some fragments and, sadly, whole sections still missing.

But I was not about to let this odyssey end badly. I slightly re-edited the chapters I had and did some light speed research to fill in the blanks. And you know what? The result of all this madness is now a much better book.

Why? Because now it had an all-important ending.

Annette had fought this disease in much the way she lived her life. She fought adversity to the bitter end. Living with MS for 26 years had not dampened her spirit. She went toe to toe with the disease and was a public advocate for research and, hopefully, a cure in her lifetime. But if that was not to be; maybe those who came after her would have a chance.

Unless you are a certain age, Annette's life is probably just a nostalgic blur. Annette's story…the Mouseketeer days, the *Beach Party* romps were all a reflection of where we were as a society. Post-war, conservative, and long held traditions and a reflection, most certainly, of a more innocent time when "happily ever after," the "white picket fence" and 2.3 children in every family was the order of the day.

The generation that revered Annette and the goodness she came to personify had dreams and fantasies. Nothing too daring or out there because that's not where America was at in that smooth sailing ride from the ''50s to the early ''60s. The revolution was still some years off, but nobody was champing at the bit for it to come.

Because they were quite content to live in the Middle American dream that was most certainly reflected by Annette.

So long story short, this updated version of the life and times of Annette Funicello tells us everything we wanted to know. The story is now complete. Something that most certainly would not have happened…

If the often erratic forces of publishing and technology had not chosen this moment to throw a wild pitch.

Annette Funicello

INTRODUCTION

OUR ROYALTY

What is the definition of royalty?

In years gone by, royalty meant station and privilege; a place and position that we could only aspire to but, realistically, never hope to achieve. Royalty never got dirty, never had problems and always lived a fairy tale life. But the concept of royalty has changed in recent years. Princess Diana saw to that.

Much in the way that Annette Funicello did.

Annette was attractive. Her black curly hair cascading down on full and enticing Italian features. That perpetual, full-mouth smile reflected youthful beauty in a chaste, childlike way. How talented she was is open to conjecture. Annette, by her own estimation "certainly wasn't the best dancer or the best singer." And, when questioned in later years about why she went on to become so popular, she was at a loss. "I guess it was just my time."

For a whole generation growing up in the '50s, a generation removed from international conflicts and the times that tried men's souls, it was also the time to be captivated by simple notions and different times. Annette Funicello helped fill the void.

Annette was the embodiment of royalty done up in a human, accessible package. She was young and wholesome. There was never a hint of negativity or cynicism. She was the '50s in all its blissed out glory. She was like us. And, in the best possible way, she played to our fantasies.

Fred Schneider of the '80s rock group The B-52's was one of those who came of age on a steady diet of Annette and, in his own hip way, summed up the intimacies between the then-child star of *The Mickey Mouse Club* and her fans. "She was like a sex goddess back when nobody had a clue."

Jerry Bowles, an author who had taken Annette and *The Mickey Mouse Club* to heart with his book *Forever Hold Your Banner High*, likewise fell in love. "I fell in love with Annette Funicello at first sight. Annette made my chest hurt. I didn't pay very much attention to her in the regular Mouseketeer sequences. But her role in *Spin and Marty* sent me into an exhalation of passion. I thought about Annette constantly."

And it was that unspoken connection, born perhaps more of naiveté and innocence than anything else, that forged the bond between Annette and our dreams.

We fell in love with Annette as we watched her sing and dance her way across *The Mickey Mouse Club* stage. She was a kid just like us. If being on the coolest television show on the planet could happen to her, it could happen to all of us. We had our first romantic stirrings as we watched Annette grow into

Annette Funicello

womanhood. In our dreams, it was possible to go on a date with her at the local malt shop and if all we got was a goodnight kiss on the cheek...well, that was the coolest.

When Annette went on to have a star-studded singing and acting career, it once again mirrored our fantasy life. And we never begrudged her the success. If we could not hang out with Paul Anka, Frankie Avalon, Fabian and Tommy Sands, then it had to be our best friend Annette who did. Because she was a real person, a decent person and a believably moral person. We watched as she married the handsome prince, began a family and lived the fairy tale happily ever after. It could not have happened any other way.

And when reality finally intruded, a divorce and later the announcement that she had MS, we cried for a while and then joined Annette, emotionally and spiritually, in her fight to recapture happiness. A second loving marriage and her continued battles to overcome her illness, continued to insure a very special place for Annette Funicello in our memories and in our hearts.

In the cold, often cynical times we live in, it is important that Annette Funicello's story be told and retold. Because good, wholesome and human are not dirty words.

Marc Shapiro 2013

CHAPTER ONE

COPING IN 1995

Annette wanted to do this real badly.

Badly enough that she was willing to forgo the comfort and surroundings of her Southern California home and experience the discomfort of a turbulent plane ride to Vancouver, Canada. Badly enough to put up with the stares and whispers of being recognized as her loving husband, Glen Holt, helped her off the plane and into a waiting wheelchair.

Annette had hoped to avoid the indignity of being wheeled through the airport, but she was not having one of her better days and so she had no choice but to accept the ride when the strength to hold up her walking cane had finally given out.

This was an offer Annette did not have to accept. She did not need the money. She definitely did not need the physical and emotional stress the trip was putting on her frail body. But the opportunity to appear as herself in the 1995 television movie about her life, *A Dream Is A Wish Your Heart Makes*, based on her 1994 autobiography of the same title, was just too much of an opportunity to pass on.

Annette Funicello

That people had liked her book had been a thrill. That Hollywood had thought enough of her life of fantasy and reality to consider making it into a movie had left her speechless.

Annette rubbed her eyes as her husband, Glen, wheeled her through the door of the soundstage, immediately plunging the couple into a dizzying patchwork quilt of darkness and scattered, light induced brightness. Crew members walked by carrying cables, camera equipment and production schedules. Some looked in her direction and smiled a friendly greeting. Some came up to her and said hello. That most of them had been born when Annette first brightened countless lives was an irony that was not lost on her.

Annette, her face drawn and tired from the flight, brightened at the idea of being on a real live movie soundstage for the first time in a long time. Glen wheeled her around a corner and onto a set where her scenes, later that day, would be shot. And into a scene that was pure fantasy.

Standing before her, dressed in white turtleneck sweaters, emblazoned with the name Annette and the classic Mouseketeer ears, were the three actresses who were playing Annette at various times in her life. Eva LaRue, who played Annette from her late teens to early '40s in the film, stepped forward and introduced Elysa Hogg, who portrayed Annette as a child and Andrea Nemeth, who is Annette during her early and middle teen years.

"Annette," happily announced LaRue and as reported in *People*, "This is your life."

Annette broke into a wide grin and laughed. Then

she cried...tears of happiness.

For actress LaRue, meeting Annette face to face for the first time was an anxious moment. She had prepared for her role as America's Sweetheart by reading and rereading her book and had watched all the Beach Party movies until she could recite the dialogue in her sleep.

"I ran up to her like I had known her for years," recalled the actress in *People* of that moment. "Then I noticed that she was looking at me really closely to see if I looked like her. I suddenly got real nervous and said 'Oops! I gotta go!' and just ran off. She must have thought I was crazy."

What LaRue would later find out was that, in Annette's eyes, she had passed the test. "Eva is everything and more than I could ask for," raved Annette in giving her personal thumbs up during that day on the set and, as reported by *People*. "I only wish I did actually look like her."

The emotional tone of *A Dream Is a Wish Your Heart Makes* changed the day Annette appeared on the set. To that point, there had been a certain detached quality surrounding the production. For many who were not familiar with Annette's story, this was just another woman's story for television. Even those who were old enough to remember Annette from her Mouseketeer days had, to that point, not formed a real emotional attachment to the story. But all that changed when Annette was wheeled onto the stage.

Suddenly the words on the script page had a flesh and blood connection. People could see the frailty and the reality of what MS could be. They could see the energy and determination present in Annette's eyes.

Annette Funicello

And, in turn, Annette could see that they really cared.

Annette had gone through all the emotional phases by 1995. There had been the moments, during those early days, when she had been scared to death at the prospect of being diagnosed with a disease that, up to that point, had no cure. There were those frantic flights after questionable attempts at cures as multiple sclerosis began to slowly but surely break down and ravage her body. But her fighting spirit and her faith in God would eventually come to the fore and, a little more than two years after she had gone public with the news that she had contracted the disease, courage and optimism had emerged as the words she now lived by.

"You learn to live with it," reflected Annette in her autobiography of her constant battle with MS. "You learn to live with anything."

But learning to live with MS was not something she came by overnight. Annette was slow to come to terms with the disease to the point where she could talk about it with anyone but the most intimate confidants. Once she went public, Annette went on a never ending search for a cure. If this had been a fairy tale, Annette would have found that cure. What she found was a lot of dead ends.

"I heard about a doctor who was giving these shots," she recalled in her book of a trip to the Bahamas in pursuit of a reported miracle cure. "But they didn't work for me. Then I was put on a steroid program that did nothing but give me insomnia. I went through acupuncture, acupressure, herbal medicines and vitamin B-12 shots. But nothing helped."

Annette's frustration continued as she fought a valiant but losing effort against the disease that, by

1993, had gone from intermittent flare ups to a constant, crippling presence in her life. Slowly she lost the ability to walk without assistance. Her equilibrium was in a constant state of imbalance, and so Annette lived, on an almost daily basis, with the fear of falling. That she finally had to give up the simple pleasure of driving was the final blow to her independence.

That she could not just hop in a car at any time and drive wherever she wanted to go was, to Annette, the ultimate humiliation and a sign that MS was leaving her in a near total state of vulnerability.

The search for a miracle cure continued. A radical experiment involving the injection of human placenta failed. Annette immediately went to the front of the line for an experimental drug called Betaseron that, in lab experiments, had been shown to reduce the frequency and severity of MS attacks. But hopes for its use were slowed down in an endless stream of government red tape. At one point, Annette was encouraged by doctors to dream and then try to remember her dreams in a radical attempt to stimulate the penal gland as a way of combating the disease. Annette, who had often stated publically that she never dreamed, tried but failed in this attempt. "I don't dream," she sighed at the memory in her book. "It would be wonderful if I could."

Trying to remain upbeat, Annette would nevertheless often express frustration at the inability to find a cure. But even in those darkest hours, she would look to the past and to happier times for strength. "Sometimes when I feel discouraged and have a problem, I find myself thinking 'If only Mr. Disney were here. He would know what to do.' And that makes me feel a little bit better," she recalled while writing her book.

Annette finally came upon a regimen of massage, physical therapy, exercise and a carefully monitored diet in 1993. While not the ultimate cure for MS, she found that she was having more "terrific days" then she had experienced in a long time. But none of the sudden progress would be worth much if Annette, along the way, had not continued with her rosy outlook on life.

"Attitude is so important," she proclaimed at the time. "When I have a bad day, I talk to myself and try to soothe over everything because I know tomorrow will be better. I've learned to enjoy life a lot more and it has certainly strengthened my faith."

As well as her resolve to remain active in both professional and charity causes.

To help educate the public about MS, Annette became an honorary spokesperson for the National Multiple Sclerosis Society and established the Annette Funicello Research Fund for Neurological Diseases. She created a successful line of designer teddy bears that she pitched on the QVC Home Shopping Network. Annette was also very hands on in the creation and marketing of her own line of perfume called Cello.

But the challenge of the moment remained her appearance in *A Dream Is a Wish Your Heart Makes*. For a sequence in which Annette was supposed to do the film's voice over narration, a task that required the concentration and timing she did not possess at that point, a voice coach, by way of a hidden microphone, talked Annette through the reading. For those who remembered Annette as the bouncy, spirited child star of *The Mickey Mouse Club* and, later, as the equally energetic teen in the Beach Party movies, this was tough to watch. Annette would start out fine, then falter, pause and finally stop as the director gently called for another take. Frustration crisscrossed her face. This should not have been that difficult she most likely thought. While knowing all along the reason it was.

Another of the brief scenes involving Annette dragged on for hours, which, when combined with the hot set, resulted in her body beginning to physically wilt under the hot lights and oppressive heat. But ever the trooper, Annette insisted on returning to the set the next day and, with the aid of ice packs on her back and legs, completed her scenes.

Watching Annette struggle and ultimately triumph in the handful of scenes of her life story proved to be an exercise in quivering lips and teary eyes from even the most hardened crew members. Actress Linda Lavin, who played Annette's mother in the film, remembered the emotional moments on that day as reported by *People*. "I don't think there was a dry eye on the set. Her life force is huge. She won't give in to this disease. "

During Annette's stay on the film set, Frankie Avalon, who was thrilled at the opportunity to play himself in a handful of scenes, arrived. When the two old friends hugged, it was like a time warp to better days had magically opened up.

Avalon, between scenes, offered to *People* that he was only too happy to play a part in Annette's cinematic life story. "I was happy to help because this was so special for her. And I liked the idea that there was no going into a character. That this was real life."

Following the completion of her final scene, Annette happily posed for publicity photos alone and with the three actresses playing the different stages of her life. There was a kind of surreal feeling when the four Annette's huddled together real close. It was as if all the struggles and all the years had finally settled into one moment of fantasy and fairy tale, to be preserved forever in time.

And when, in the aftermath of the photo shoot, the four Annette's broke into a spontaneous rendition of the "*Mickey Mouse Club* Theme Song", the impact of her life and times seemed to finally, and positively, come home to Annette.

She smiled a big smile. Then she started to cry.

CHAPTER TWO

THE ROAD TO CALIFORNIA

One of the few constants in Utica, New York, during the early 1940s was Rocky's Diner.

It was a place where you could get an honest meal at an honest price and good conversation from the genial owner, Rocco "Rocky" Albano and any of a number of blue collar working people of the town who frequented this bastion of all things Italian. And so it was, as the clouds of World War II began gathering over the United States and the rest of the world, Rocky's Diner was the place where a local mechanic named Joseph Funicello first laid eyes on a beautiful restaurant hostess named Virginia Albano.

Joseph made a point of coming into Rocky's every Sunday. It was the place where he would eat a hearty breakfast and meet, informally, with the people he owed money to and pay them off. Joseph was known for his shyness and for being a man of a few words. And so rather than boldly approaching her for her name, her telephone number and a date, Joseph Funicello was content to admire Virginia Albano from afar.

Virginia recalled noticing Joseph but not paying too much attention to him. He seemed nice enough in a ruggedly, salt of the earth kind of way. But Virginia was picky. She would not strike up an acquaintance with just any man. When Joseph would speak of his interest in Virginia, which was rare, it was usually as an aside to Rocco who would listen intently but say very little.

And smile as he took the news of Joseph's interest back to his sister.

Virginia took the news with little enthusiasm. She had been brought up a strict Catholic and so was true to the edict that she could not date Jewish boys. What she failed to realize was that Funicello was an Italian name.

Joseph continued to pine away for Virginia, paying regular visits to Rocky's Diner and bending Rocco's ear about his feelings for Virginia. One day Joseph, with a bit of bravado, pointed to Virginia working behind the counter and said, as reported in Annette's autobiography, "Someday I'm going to marry her." Rocky busted out laughing and revealed that Virginia was his sister. Joseph, incredulous and somewhat embarrassed, did not believe him.

As Annette would document in her book many years later, Rocky yelled across the restaurant for Virginia to come over. He reportedly said, "You're my sister, right?" When she replied yes, Rocky added to Joseph's embarrassment when he said, "Joe says he's going to marry you someday." Virginia laughed and said, "We'll see about that." But sharp eyed patrons at Rocky's Diner that day also noticed something else. A very real smile from Virginia in the direction of Joseph that indicated some interest.

What followed was months and months of a cat and mouse courtship in which the shy Joseph courted and eventually, reported Virginia, "Little by little he wore me down. But as Joseph and Virginia's love blossomed, there were other considerations.

There were legitimate fears that their respective parents would not approve of their love. They were both quite young and, in Virginia's parents' eyes, Joseph was a suspect catch. He was working and had the reputation in the community as an honest man. But who knew for sure and, with the US about to enter World War II, there was the fear that the winds of war might separate them shortly after they married, and so they counseled their daughter to move slowly.

But in a move that flew in the face of their strict family upbringings, Joseph and Virginia approached a friend who also happened to be a priest. He agreed to secretly marry them and, on April 17, 1941, Joseph and Virginia became husband and wife.

For the next five months the newlyweds continued to live a double life. They continued to live at their parents' homes and would have to make elaborate plans to get away and be together. It was romantic but all the secrecy and stress involved in keeping their secret was beginning to put a strain on the new marriage, and so finally they called their families together and broke the news to them.

There was some disappointment that they had cheated their parents out of throwing a big Italian wedding but it was a disappointment that all but disappeared, shortly before Christmas, when they announced that Virginia was pregnant.

Annette Funicello

Annette Joanne Funicello was born October 22, 1942. The first grandchild on either side of the family and the only girl among the Funicello/Albano cousins, Annette was the immediate center of attention. Aunts and uncles would regularly disrupt Virginia's carefully planned eating and sleeping schedule for her newborn with unexpected snacks and playtimes, which resulted in Annette recalling her childhood as one in which she was never eating, never sleeping and always whining and crying.

Annette recalled spending those early years "loved, wanted and being the typical spoiled brat." Joseph would often come home from a hard day's work to find his house a veritable circus in which Virginia was attempting to put their daughter down for a nap while relatives were doing everything possible to entertain the young child and keep her awake. Those were battles of will that Virginia rarely won and, on more than one occasion, would good naturedly throw up her hands and say she was ready to throw Annette out a window.

While not growing up in a particularly musical household, Annette, quite naturally, gravitated toward music. There was something in the way the very young child moved in time to music heard on the radio and on records and how she reacted to certain sound patterns that appeared almost uncanny to her parents. And music was something that was encouraged.

She was never far from the family record player, and when the radio was on in the living room, Annette could be found standing or sitting nearby, singing along with the hits of the day. A song that Annette was particularly fond of was "Accentuate the Positive."

While she admitted in later years to being to being extremely shy, Annette could be coaxed into impromptu singing performances in front of her parents and large circle of relatives.

Joseph Funicello managed to avoid being drafted into the military by virtue of his status as a husband and father. A second child, Joey Funicello, was born in 1945. Joseph's reputation as a topflight mechanic was providing his growing family with a good, no frills yet comfortable blue collar life.

But Joseph and Virginia were not satisfied.

The couple remained romantics at heart who yearned for the grand adventure. They were not the couple to let little things like family and responsibility get in their way, and the cold weather of Utica was not to their liking. The fantasy that was sunny Southern California finally proved too strong a lure, and so, early in 1946, Joseph and Virginia once again called their families together and announced that Joseph was selling his mechanic business and the family was moving to California.

Their families were once again less than thrilled with the couple's latest pronouncement. They were concerned.

One relative warned, and years later reported by Annette in telling her story, that the Funicello family would "die lousy in California." Others told them that they were throwing away everything on an impossible dream. But Joseph and Virginia could not be dissuaded, and so, in August 1946, with no prospects for a job, a home or ties to family and friends, they tucked Annette and Joey into the back seat of the family's 1940 Dodge and, with a trailer full of belongings hitched to the back, they set out on the road to California.

The projected three-week trip to California was shaping up to be a dream adventure for the non-traditional, risk taking Funicellos. But the dream quickly turned into a nightmare. They had counted on erratic weather, especially during the Midwestern leg of their journey. What they had not counted on was the modern day equivalent of the biblical ten plagues.

During one of their frequent rest stops, Joey fell out of his high chair and hit his head on the curb. The Funicellos anguished over the injuries that might be serious or fatal. Annette recalled what happened next. "I developed a case of chicken pox so severe that I could not swallow food."

Not surprisingly Joey also caught the chicken pox. Joseph and Virginia were forced to hide their children in the car when they stopped at drive in restaurants because a waitress, seeing the children with the illness, would refuse to serve them. The Dodge inevitably had its run of mechanical problems that added to their quickly depleting money, and the emotional dark clouds that were gathering over the Funicello's trip west.

Virginia was feeling particularly homesick, and, in their lowest moments, the couple seriously considered turning around and heading back to Utica. However, Annette would recall in later years that her parents were made of sterner stuff and that their pioneer spirit and a search for their dreams and a better life kept them going.

And Joseph and Virginia knew they would not get either by turning around and going back to Utica.

The Funicello family overcame the obstacles and eventually found themselves looking out on the Los Angeles skyline for the first time in early September. The euphoria of having survived the hardships and arriving in the land of opportunity would be short-lived as the reality of having no job, very little money and no place to live settled over the family. Still the Funicello family was more excited at their prospects for the future than the immediate challenges they faced.

"We didn't worry, we were happy," remembered Virginia of those first days in Los Angeles. "We had each other and we had our two babies. That's all we needed."

But money was, in fact, very tight, and so the Funicello's first home turned out to be a trailer park in a less than desirable part of Los Angeles. Annette's memories of the trailer park stay were few and unpleasant. Many of the other park families did not cotton to the idea of an Italian family in their midst, and so the family, especially Annette and Joey, were isolated from the rest of the park residents.

On the up side, mechanics were very much in demand during the late '40s, and so it was not long before Joseph had found work and was able to move his family to a small house in North Hollywood and, eventually, to a home on Valley Spring Lane in the Los Angeles suburb of Studio City.

The Funicello family's arrival in Studio City coincided with a change in demeanor in Annette. Overnight the self-centered spoiled child evolved into a well behaved, well-mannered girl who her mother would often compliment by calling her an angel. But one thing that did not change was Annette's acute shyness.

The day she was dropped off for her first day of kindergarten was traumatic for the young child who had never been in the company of anyone but family. On that first day of school, a terrified Annette held onto her father so tightly that she ripped the buttons right off his shirt. Joseph eventually convinced his daughter to go inside, but she insisted that he stand outside the classroom for several days until she felt secure enough to endure school on her own.

Annette eventually came out of her shell and began to interact with other children and to be an active participant in school despite the fact she was often reluctant to raise her hand in class. Her nervous energy, coupled with her insecurities, would often manifest themselves in Annette nervously tapping her fingers and toes in the classroom. It was a habit that was not lost on her kindergarten teacher, who saw that the youngster had an instinctive sense of rhythm.

During a parent-teacher conference the teacher brought this bit of information to the attention of Virginia, assuring Annette's mother that her daughter's natural rhythm was a gift and suggesting she introduce a musical instrument into her daughter's life. When Virginia approached Annette with the idea, Annette readily agreed and excitedly said that she wanted to play the drums.

Annette took to the instrument and showed surprising dexterity for a five-year-old. A music teacher was hired, and the early slamming and crashing of sticks on drum skins soon gave way to ambitious, rhythmic patterns. Joseph and Virginia would often watch with growing pride and no small amount of amusement, as Annette, barely visible behind the huge drum kit with drum sticks flailing above her head, would beat out a difficult rhythm. In due course, she would add the xylophone to her list of musical skills.

News of Annette's emerging talents soon spread outside the family home and around the neighborhood. Margaret Rix, who lived a few doors down from the Funicellos, ran a local dance school. She suggested to Virginia that Annette needed to be around kids and that dancing lessons might be the answer. Virginia agreed that dance lessons might help her daughter come out of her shell. Annette seemed reluctant at first. But when a school mate named Jackie, who was already taking lessons, suggested Annette give it a try, she agreed to give dance lessons a shot. After the first lesson Annette was hooked.

A whole new world opened up to Annette in the next four years. Encouraged by her skills as a dancer, she began to come out of her shell amid a growing circle of friends. When not learning the intricacies of tap, ballet and the hula, Annette would indulge herself in the normal childhood pursuits of biking, skating and clowning around at neighborhood pool parties.

The Funicello family continued to be that much needed refuge of warmth. Sunday was considered family day. After attending St. Cyril's Catholic Church in the morning, the family would pile into their car and drive to the beach or the mountains for a picnic. After arriving in California, the family would make occasional trips back to Utica during the summer, cementing Annette's ties with her grandparents, aunts,

Annette Funicello

uncles and cousins.

And while her dance and music instruction remained an important part of her life, Annette had seemingly no interest in a show business career. "I was going to dance classes everyday and I wanted to be a ballerina. But that was as far as it was going to go," she recalled in her book.

But forces were at work that would lead her away from anything resembling a "normal life."

Her natural ability had soon made her a standout in Margaret Rix's class, with Annette quickly advancing from group routines to featured soloist. By age nine, her shy nature had become a natural adjunct to her musical and dancing talents and, when combined with a natural charming personality, resulted in her winning a local beauty pageant and the title of Miss Willow Lake. Which led to some early modeling assignments that showcased the young girl's ease and comfort in front of the camera.

In 1955, Annette accepted an invitation to join the Burbank dance troop Ballet vs. Jive, headed by local dance instructor Al Gilbert. One of her first dance routines with Ballet vs. Jive was as the lead in a production of *Swan Lake*, staged outdoors at the Burbank Bowl. That night, it was overcast and threatening rain as the young girl stepped to the front of the stage and put on a dazzling display of footwork and coordination that ended with a thunderous round of applause.

What Annette did not know was that a man named Disney was sitting in the audience. He had been invited to the concert to see his friend conduct the orchestra. What he had not intended was to be

Marc Shapiro

knocked off his feet by Annette's performance.

The next day the telephone rang at the Funicello house. Representatives for Walt Disney were on the line. They wanted to meet with Annette. It was not an unexpected call.

Shortly after the conclusion of the Burbank show, Al Gilbert had received a phone call from the Disney Studio inquiring about Annette. Gilbert immediately called Virginia and Annette with what he considered good news. He was sure they would share his enthusiasm for the opportunity.

"We didn't know what an audition was," recalled Virginia. "We were not sure we wanted to be bothered with it."

But Gilbert persisted, saying it would be a feather in his cap if she went in and that he would help prepare her for the dance portion of the audition. Virginia felt a loyalty to Gilbert, and the idea of visiting a movie studio did seem like it would be fun. And so Annette finally agreed to give the audition a try.

Knowing full well that it would probably not lead to anything.

CHAPTER THREE

I CAN'T SING...
YOU'RE HIRED

It was pouring rain the day Annette was driven by her mother to the Walt Disney Studios in nearby Burbank for her initial audition for *The Mickey Mouse Club*. The weather conditions matched her mood.

Dark and cloudy.

Annette was thrilled when she heard the news that Walt Disney, the creator of Mickey Mouse, Donald Duck and a literal tidal wave of her favorite cartoon and movie characters, wanted her to audition for his new singing/dancing/variety show. Her parents were thrilled and were immediately on the phone to Utica, excitedly telling family and relatives that their daughter was about to get her big show business break. But once the initial excitement died down, Annette's old fears and insecurities began to return. She did not get much sleep the night before the audition...

And then announced that she did not want to go.

Virginia was in a quandary. She knew this was a once in a lifetime opportunity that would most certainly change her daughter's life. But she could also sense the consequences of forcing her daughter to go to the audition and then failing to get the part. Finally she went to her daughter with a bit of child psychology. She told Annette she did not have to do anything she did not want to do. Annette thought about it for a moment and said that she would go to the studio.

Her fears subsided somewhat as her mother drove through the gates of the Burbank studio. She stared wide-eyed at the place where her dreams were made. She giggled when she spotted street signs naming various locales on the Disney lot after her favorite cartoon characters. Annette's fears began to melt away.

Those fears returned when she walked into the audition room and found it filled to overflowing with children and their mothers. Annette and her mother sat in a corner of the waiting room and silently listened to show business shop talk from the others at the audition. Annette's confidence took a further hit when she realized that all the other children looked alike but that none of them looked like her. On the surface, it appeared that Annette was as far from show business material as any child could be.

What she could not have realized was that her inexperience and innocence was exactly what Walt Disney was looking for.

Disney wanted ordinary kids, preferably with little or no show business experience. He felt that it was more important that the Mouseketeers, the group that would be starring in his new venture, be able to get along during the long hours of rehearsal and performance and learn on the job rather than having to deal with polished performers and show business egos.

Consequently the casting process for *The Mickey Mouse Club* had turned into a long, drawn out process. By the time Annette walked into the audition room, Disney and his producers had looked at more than 3,000 children and, at that point, had selected 23.

Annette's personality and charm instantly won over Disney, producer Bill Walsh and the adult Mouseketeer mentors Jimmy Dodd and Roy Williams. Annette was invited back for a second audition. Privately those privy to the audition were shocked that she had made it through the first round. The consensus was that Annette had a nice smile and a sweet personality but not much else.

But there was no getting around the fact that Walt Disney liked her a lot.

During her call back, Annette continued to dazzle with her dancing ability and the novelty of a nine-year-old girl beating out fantastic rhythms on the drums. She was called back for a third and final audition. Annette's confidence level had grown by leaps and bounds. She suddenly felt she had a chance.

But one final obstacle remained in her path.

"On the third time he [Walt Disney] asked me if I could sing," recalled Annette in later years. "I said no. He said that was too bad, but then he said that everybody can sing."

Annette was crestfallen. But rather than dismiss her, she was encouraged by Disney to try. She took a deep breath and began to sing the Jaye P. Morgan classic "That's All I Want from You." Disney listened intently for a few moments and then asked her to try something else. Annette thought about it for a moment, most likely assuming this would be her last chance, and began to sing "The Ballad of Davey Crockett." She completed the song, Disney thanked her and the audition was over.

Annette left the Disney Studios with mixed feelings. She felt she had done her best, but that the lack of a singing voice would ultimately derail her chances.

A couple of days later the telephone rang with the news that Annette was being signed to a two-week tryout contract with the blue team (the second string of Mouseketeer performers) to see how she would adjust to the grind of a television series and, more importantly, how she got along with her fellow cast members.

Walt Disney's confidence in Annette was not echoed by other members of the production staff, who predicted that she would be gone in two weeks, largely based on her seeming inability to perform the more elaborate dance routines that would be required. And then there was her singing, which was marginal at best.

Mouseketeer Tommy Cole was among those who did not see Annette hanging around long based on talent alone, as chronicled in *Forever Hold Your Banner High*. "She was just a plain, flat-chested little girl in the beginning. But Annette was handpicked by Disney, and so everybody felt she would be around for a while."

Cole's prediction that Annette would make the grade came true. Walt Disney had taken an immediate liking to the dark curly-haired child with the exotic looks. Consequently the last of the 24 original

Annette Funicello

Mouseketeers to be signed, and the only one personally picked by Disney, was signed for the then outrageous sum of $160 a week. Within a week, Annette had been promoted from the blue team to the frontline red team.

The seven-year contract offered Annette seemed fair. It contained many pages of legal mumbo jumbo and fine print that was confusing to Annette and her parents. What they did understand was money, and what the contract projected was substantial increases to $325 a week salary in 1959 and $500 a week by 1962. Joseph and Virginia felt it was the right thing to do, and so, without consulting a lawyer or an agent, signed on the bottom line.

Annette soon found herself inside the Disney Studios wardrobe department, where she gazed for the first time upon the blue skirt, white shirt and black mouse ears that would be like a second skin during the run of the show. Her first impressions of the Mouseketeer uniform were mixed. She could live with the skirt and the shirt (although she did have some questions about how they were going to get her name on it), but she felt the mouse ears were silly and unglamorous.

Annette's apprehension about *The Mickey Mouse Club* quickly dissolved as she settled into the six day a week, 9 to 5 working days in preparation for the October 1955 premiere. From the outset Disney intended to make things easy for his young charges.

The schedule reflected a non-entertainment, real world schedule. They would rehearse for three days and then film for three days. Given the lack of show business pretense, Annette came quickly out of her shell and made fast friends with the rest of the cast members. The more experienced show biz kids found something refreshing in Annette's innocence. They were extremely patient and supportive in guiding her through the realities of television and quick to answer her questions.

She developed particularly strong bonds with her two grown up Mouseketeers, Jimmy and Roy, who, when on the set, came to be her surrogate parents. Jimmy, in particular, had a knack for knowing when Annette was having a rough moment and was quick to her side to say or do just the right thing to calm her down or point her in the right direction.

Annette's natural affinity for dressing up and pretending made the multiple costume changes and the number of dance routines that would make up the lions share of each episode a relatively easy chore. Annette was still unsure of her singing talents, and Disney sensibly did not rush her into the spotlight. She would occasionally take a short lead in a song or dance number, but in the beginning she gained confidence through participating in group songs.

When not rehearsing or filming, Annette and the others would keep up with their studies in a mobile trailer with on-set teacher Jean Seaman. The classroom environment was as normal as it could be given the circumstances. Age appropriate studies and homework assignments were taught daily. The only thing that made studio school unpredictable was the fact that the children would often be called out of class to film and rehearse.

It was all new and exciting for Annette. She acknowledged working hard but was quick to say that

Annette Funicello

she woke up each morning with a smile on her face.

Which was not to say that life during those early days on *The Mickey Mouse Club* were stress-free for Annette and her family.

To his credit, Disney bent over backwards to make life on the set as normal as possible for his young charges. He visited the set daily, inquiring how everybody was doing and if everything was alright. The children, as part of the Disney control package, appeared periodically before the California State Board of Health where they were weighed and interviewed to determine if they were eating well and getting enough rest. Annette's mother was interviewed as well to determine if her daughter was exhibiting any symptoms of stress. Visits to the Board of Health were always terror-filled moments for Virginia, who feared that her daughter would, somehow, not pass the examinations.

Disney was also adamant that the Mouseketeers keep up their grades and warned the kids that they would not be able to work if their grades fell below a certain level.

But easily the biggest impact on the life on Annette and her family was the stipulation that a parent or guardian be on the lot every minute of their child's working day and that, for insurance purposes, siblings were not allowed on the set. At the time, Joseph was working six days and sometimes seven days a week at a San Fernando Valley garage, and so the burden of supervising the family fell to Virginia. Annette's younger brother, Joseph, had just entered grade school but the latest addition to the Funicello clan, Michael, had just turned two.

With few friends and nobody she really trusted, Virginia turned to Michael's godmother, who willingly took Michael during the day. The drastic change in the family's routine did not set well with Michael, who would cry constantly until he got used to the new routine. Michael was not the only one who had to adjust to Annette's new entertainment life.

Virginia, laboring under the threat of Annette's contract being canceled if Virginia were caught leaving the studio during her daughter's work day, would often risk Annette's career to run home to start dinner and go shopping. When Joseph got off work, he would pick up Michael, go home and continue dinner preparations so that the evening meal would be ready when Annette and Virginia got home.

Annette and the rest of the Mouseketeers continued to mold themselves into a cohesive entertainment unit. The Disney approach to creating a television show was fairly simple: Show up on time, know your lines and follow directions. Admittedly this was often a tough line for this group of children to toe, and a few of the performers were dismissed early in the rehearsal stage when they could not follow those simple instructions. On the other hand, Annette's temperament seemed ideally suited to this regimented environment. She began showing signs in those early days of stepping out from the crowd and into the spotlight.

By May, Annette and her Mouseketeer co-stars were learning firsthand the reality of making a daily one-hour television show. They were getting a lot of the stand-alone segments of the show taped and in the can well in advance of the premiere of the show.

Annette would often acknowledge that it could be confusing not knowing when or in which episode a particular segment would appear. What she was quite clear about was the first time she stepped before the camera for the first time in a *Mickey Mouse Club* segment called "Talent Roundup," dressed in a fringed western outfit and a cowboy hat. For Annette it was truly a magical moment.

The year 1955 was a banner year for Walt Disney on a number of fronts. Not only was there excitement and anticipation at the prospect of *The Mickey Mouse Club* going on the air but Disney also chose that year to officially open his long-anticipated amusement park, Disneyland. And so it was, on July 17, 1955, during the star-studded opening ceremonies for the park, that the Mouseketeers made their first public appearance.

Annette and the rest of the Mouseketeers stood nervously backstage as the live television special, co-hosted by Ronald Reagan, Bob Cummings and Art Linkletter, beamed the wonders of Disney's Magic Kingdom into living rooms across the nation.

Backstage Jimmy Dodd and Roy Williams were doing their best to calm the children, but it was to no avail as they were totally caught up in the excitement of the moment. And the fact that they were mere moments away from meeting the public for the first time.

At the tail end of the line, Annette was particularly nervous. All they had to do was march out in a single file and yell out their names. "How hard could that be?" she asked herself. Still, she silently practiced yelling out her name as the moment neared.

Finally Jimmy stepped to the microphone and shouted for the first time "Mouseketeer roll call! Count off now!" *The Mickey Mouse Club* stepped out smartly and, amid thunderous applause and the popping of camera flashbulbs, enthusiastically marched to the microphone and shouted out their names. When her turn finally came, Annette stepped up and shouted...

"Annette!"

Bob Cummings returned to the stage as the applause continued and, in the spirit of the moment, predicted, "I guarantee many a future star will come out of this group."

Annette smiled. She liked the sound of that.

CHAPTER FOUR

THE WONDER YEAR

In 1955, only 60 percent of American households had a television set. And it was a safe bet that a good many of them were tuned in when *The Mickey Mouse Club* premiered on October 3, 1955.

For Annette and her family, the weeks leading up to *The Mickey Mouse Club's* premiere was a blur of excitement. Annette and the others were constantly at the studio, taping segments and fine tuning dance routines. The public relations push had begun and the Mouseketeers, many for the first time, were faced with doing press interviews and posing for pictures. Annette remained shy in the face of newspaper and magazine inquiries and tended to fade into the background during group interviews and let the more outgoing members of the cast do the talking.

At home, Annette was being bombarded with questions from neighbors and excited telephone calls from her relatives in Utica. Annette laughingly signed her first autographs. Virginia was quietly enthusiastic, the thrill having been softened by her constant presence at the studio. But Joseph, Joey and Michael had been getting all the news secondhand up to this point, and so their level of enthusiasm was high and, in the case of Joseph, very supportive and in many ways childlike.

Finally the big day arrived. Disney had allowed the children to leave the studio early that day so they could watch the very first episode in the comfort of their homes with their families. Annette and her family anxiously sat forward in their seats as the first images of *The Mickey Mouse Club* logo flickered onto their tiny television screen. At the first sight of Annette in the opening number, Annette recalled that her father was completely overwhelmed and emotional to the point of tears.

The Mickey Mouse Club's mixture of educational and entertainment features, with theme days, song and dance numbers and daily exposure to classic Disney cartoons, proved an instant critical winner with reviewers falling all over themselves in praise of this latest phase of the Disney family entertainment empire.

This early in the life of the show, no one member of the cast was emerging from the rest of the Mouseketeers as a stand out. But privately there was already a growing support from those privy to the day to day operation of the show that there was a glimmer of something special in Annette.

The typical work day on the set of *The Mickey Mouse Club* was low key. There were rarely fits of show business temper or ego, and those were quickly dealt with. A handful of Mouseketeers were reprimanded during the first season when their attitudes threatened to disrupt the harmony of the

Annette Funicello

show. Disney was so intent on keeping problems from arising that he deliberately withheld fan mail from his young charges, lest the perceived popularity of certain cast members over others cause ego problems.

And Disney's edict of positive vibes reportedly extended to the attitudes of crew members.

Annette would recall with a sense of wonder that any crew members caught swearing or even using the word "damn" on the set in front of the children would be fired the next day.

Annette's story of crewmen being reprimanded for using profanity would be contradicted years later by former Mouseketeer Lonnie Burr in his autobiography *Confessions of an Accidental Mouseketeer*. "Annette's story about being fired for saying 'damn' is not true. We used and heard a lot worse words than that."

The reality of life on *The Mickey Mouse Club* set was that these were children. And so it was not too surprising to discover that there were spats and that this group of child actors did not always get along. Name calling was not uncommon and, despite Disney's best efforts, cliques did form between certain segments of the cast. Unknown to Disney, the backbiting often centered on a cast member's talent or lack of same. The reason Disney was in the dark about many disputes was that, like most children, the Mouseketeers chose to settle it among themselves.

Annette remembered the day when, shortly before the curtain was set to rise on a song and dance number, a cast mate snuck up behind her and smeared her makeup. There was no time to fix it, and so Annette went on with makeup smeared all over her face.

Uncharacteristically, Annette was furious at the prank, but the incident was ultimately forgotten when everybody, including Annette, busted out laughing.

The makeup smearing incident may well have been a childish bit of jealousy at the fact that Annette, despite Disney's insistence that everybody on the show was of equal stature, was slowly but surely emerging as the star attraction. For her part, Annette never gave the impression that she was better than anybody else. But, in a moment of candor, she did concede that she might have an edge.

"Maybe it was the mop of black curls that set me apart from the other girls," speculated Annette in her autobiography. "The other 23 Mouseketeers were certainly better singers and dancers than I was. I was the only ethnic looking one in the group while everyone else was All American looking. Which was the way I wanted to look."

What Annette would never go into was the fact that there was real friction early on between Annette and fellow Mouseketeer Darlene Gillespie. Darlene, one of the older members of the cast, was also considered one of the most talented and, by consensus of the other Mouseketeers, more talented than Annette. Consequently when the first signs of favoritism toward Annette began to emerge, Darlene and her parents began to complain.

Former Mouseketeer Bobby Burgess agreed, saying in *Forever Hold Your Banner High,* "The studio had begun to push Annette, and Darlene and her parents began to complain."

In later years, Darlene would downplay the alleged feud that was taking place at the time. She would clarify that all of the stories about feuds between Annette and her were primarily caused by "stage parents" who were attempting to make everything into a competition. In fact the only thing that Darlene could remember causing any problem between the two girls was the fact that Annette got new tap shoes, and Darlene was left with an old used pair.

Alleged feuds aside, Disney knew that Annette, rather than Darlene or Cubby as many had predicted, was definitely coming into her own as the star Mouseketeer. That Annette had been handpicked by Disney had immediately set her apart. Other members of the Mouseketeer cast were not surprised when Disney's favorite began to lead the pack.

"Annette was warm and natural when she acted," reflected Bobby Burgess in *The Mickey Mouse Club Scrapbook*. "And people tended to be drawn to that."

Doreen Tracy indicated in *Forever Hold Your Banner High* and several newspaper interviews in later years that Disney's promotion of Annette was more mercenary than that. "I think Annette was the most saleable product Disney had at the time. The whole Italian thing was hot at the time and Annette, in Disney's eyes, was like a small version of Sophia Loren. Annette stood out. She had that little extra bit of charisma, and that's what sells. Most of us were out there hamming it up, but Annette never overacted and that's what drew attention to her."

Lonnie Burr agreed that Annette's rise to prominence had more to do with behind the scenes manipulation than any perceived talent. "I don't think she had any particular magic. What she had was exposure."

Disney would always deny he had a favorite and would dance around the notion that The Mickey Mouse Club would ultimately produce stars. "These are just regular American kids," Disney would often say in interviews. "There isn't a show off among them. The most remarkable thing about the Mouseketeers is their normalcy."

However, pundits who would continue to examine *The Mickey Mouse Club* and Annette for years after the show went to syndication heaven, seemed, at the time, to have Disney's feelings about Annette pegged.

The qualities of honesty, sweetness, spirituality and, most intriguing, virginity clung to her like a fairy tale gown. For an estimated five million pre-teen viewers, Annette was the fantasy. She was the one you wanted to sneak around and do romantic things with and, at the same time, she was the one you wanted to marry. Annette was quite simply the personification of a dream.

Despite public comments to the contrary, the reality was that Walt Disney was a good businessman, and he knew that as far as *The Mickey Mouse Club* went, Annette was the uncrowned star of the show. And so as the first season progressed, he began, in subtle and not so subtle ways, to retool scripts and regular segments to feature her. Thinking long term and to a relationship with Annette that might well outlast the life of the show, he made the move midway through the first season to create a serial for the show, essentially a movie chopped into segments to run on *The Mickey Mouse Club* and starring Annette, entitled

Annette Funicello

Adventures In Dairyland.

On the surface, *Adventures In Dairyland* was a fairly simple, kid friendly tale in which Annette, playing herself, and child actor Sammy Ogg travel to Wisconsin where, as the guests of a farm family and their three children, they learn how to run a dairy farm and, along the way, have the expected adventures, misadventures and, in the case of Annette, a first chaste brush with romance with the farmer's oldest son. Despite her time on *The Mickey Mouse Club,* Annette looked at *Adventures In Dairyland* as the first time she was really acting.

Adventures In Dairyland would prove to be a big step in expanding the scope of The *Mickey Mouse Club*. To that point any location shooting for the first season serials had been filmed on the Disney sound stages or at nearby Los Angeles locations. But Disney insisted that *Adventures In Dairyland* be filmed on a real Wisconsin farm, and so Annette and her mother were soon on their way to the tiny hamlet of Verona, Wisconsin, for four weeks of shooting.

These were already trying times for Annette and her family. But Joseph and the rest of the family had adjusted fairly well to having a star in their midst. There were no complaints when Annette's father would have to race home during his workday to attend to household chores. Joe and Michael were at an age when they only saw the disruptions and a lack of a normal schedule as one big adventure.

But for Virginia, Annette's sudden thrust into celebrity was proving an emotional, often trying experience. Before *The Mickey Mouse Club*, the relationship between Virginia and Annette was that of a typical mother and daughter. Things were settled quickly and easily.

But with the advent of the television show, show business and celebrity obligations had become no less important in their relationship. Annette's chores around the house often had to be scheduled around the filming of the show or homework. Family meals were often late or in shifts, especially when Michael was often asleep by the time Annette and Virginia got home from the studio. Virginia was happy with her daughter's success, but it was a difficult adjustment to make.

Consequently the prospect of being away from home and on the other side of the country for an extended period of time had mother and daughter in a mixed frame of mind as they packed their bags and gave Joseph specific instructions for feeding the children and himself, making sure the boys were picked up from school by the babysitter and to schedule a house cleaner.

The month in Verona was a full plate of activity. There were long days of filming in which the city girl Annette had the chance to milk cows, feed calves, chase after escaped pigs and make jelly. During the time away from the set, Annette and her mother would walk the streets of Verona, visit the shops and eat in quaint restaurants. It was a wonderful experience for mother and daughter, but one that saw mother and daughter missing the family and hating the idea of having to travel long distances from home to work. This trait would follow Annette in later years.

Annette returned to Los Angeles and the well-oiled machine that *The Mickey Mouse Club* had

Annette Funicello

become. Her life revolved the show, and so it came as no surprise that Annette's really close relationships developed within the cast. Two of the closest were with Sharon Baird and Bobby Burgess. It was also during this period that Annette, who had by this time turned 10, had her first childhood romance with another Mouseketeer Lonnie Burr.

Burr, in looking back on that special time with Annette in *Forever Hold Your Banner High*, dismissed it as "puppy love romance." What was significant about their relationship was that it was the first sign of Annette's budding womanhood and, not surprisingly, her parents were not thrilled. In particular, Joseph was disapproving of Annette pairing off with Lonnie. And when Mouseketeer John Lee Johann started a rumor that Annette was seen kissing Bobby Burgess behind a trailer, Virginia was quick to corner the young rumor monger in the middle of the Disney Studio lot and yell at him for making up stories.

Annette and Lonnie were typical of the infatuations that had developed among the group of child actors. A lot of hand holding, a friendship ring and, in the case of Annette and Lonnie, a very first romantic kiss. There were also the fights, the breakups and the makeups. All of which Annette experienced with Lonnie.

Disney, despite the fact that no Mouseketeer was older than 14 and most were under 12, made sure that any pairings were well supervised and that at least one if not both mothers were always around when his Mouseketeers paired off. Because even at the puppy love stage, he knew how easily romantic issues could disrupt a working relationship.

Annette made one of her closest and longest lasting friendships when she met and became fast friends with young actress Shelley Fabares. They were the perfect emotional match, the same age and the same shy temperament. Shelley was somebody Annette could confide her deepest thoughts to.

Especially when it came to stardom, which, as the first season of *The Mickey Mouse Club* began to wind down, had become a two-edged sword. One of the perks of being on *The Mickey Mouse Club* was that Annette was given free access to Disneyland. She was allowed to go to the front of the line. Yes, she was recognized, mobbed and approached for autographs. But in this public fantasy setting Annette was relatively comfortable in the spotlight.

It was when she hung up her ears and attempted to just be Annette that she would run into obstacles in her attempts to have a normal life. Shopping trips and family nights out at a restaurant would regularly turn into mob scenes. Annette could not even go to church without being approached for an autograph. Neighbors were knocking on her door at all hours, and her brother Joey had even taken to selling their telephone number to his friends.

Annette would do her best to present the best possible face to this fan frenzy. But it was obvious from the tight smile and the "deer caught in the headlights" look in her eyes that had become her public face that the little girl behind the Mickey Mouse ears and the perky smile was becoming increasingly uncomfortable with these intrusions.

Annette would often admit that being in the public eye was a challenge, that it was not her nature

Annette Funicello

to be outgoing and that away from the studio she just wanted to be herself. Annette, in the wake of stardom, was still very much an introverted child. Shelley continued to be her closest friend outside the studio, and it was with her, spending time at each other's homes, talking on the phone, gossiping and playing records, that Annette found escape and the chance to be normal.

The first season of *The Mickey Mouse Club* was nearing its conclusion. And it was obvious that Annette was the star. Fan mail favoring Annette was running into the hundreds of letters a day, heart-warming proposals of marriage from young boys and a lot of "we think you're great" sentiments. And because Annette's popularity by that time was really not a secret, Disney felt comfortable enough in the cast's togetherness that he went to the set one day to discuss fan mail with his cast, in particular the amount that Annette was getting.

Behind the scenes, the fan mail issue kicked up a storm. More than one studio employee indicated that until the fan mail started coming in, everybody had expected Cubby to emerge as the star of the show. Others speculated that the massive amount of letters had, in fact, been written by Annette's family and relatives.

Lonnie Burr stopped short of confirming the fact in *Confessions of an Accidental Mouseketeer*, but he said if the rumors were true, it would not surprise him. "There was the rumor that Annette and her parents had written all her relatives and had them write fan letters to the show and that, because of that, she was beginning to get more parts. It could be because

Disney tended to measure things in terms of mail response."

Annette tended to ignore those rumors and was thrilled that the public had chosen to single her out. The fan mail validated a lot of the fantasies she had long harbored about being a star. But the excitement was quickly replaced by concern that she would be ostracized by her television friends because she had emerged as the fan favorite. It was an internal conflict. The desire for popularity weighed against the ramifications of popularity. At her lowest, Annette would often wish she could just melt back into the cast again and just be one of 24.

Annette's growing popularity would have its dark side.

There were the occasional strange fan letters that, despite Disney's best efforts to shield her, would fall into Annette's hands. There was also the day a disturbed fan with a knife, screaming "Annette! Annette!" was intercepted outside the Disney Studio gates.

On an early promotional tour, Annette's sharp-eyed mother spotted a young man lurking suspiciously in the hotel lobby and alerted security. As the young man was being led away, he let it be known to anyone who would listen that he was at the hotel to hurt Annette.

Annette was surprisingly calm in the face of these very real threats, but she was beginning to realize that there was a fine line between fan and fanatic and that it would be in her best interest to learn the difference and become aware of the telltale signs.

With the conclusion of the first season, the

Annette Funicello

Mouseketeers were allowed to return to some semblance of the real world. With their set tutors now on vacation, Annette and the others were allowed to return to public school. It had been nearly two years since Annette had been with children other than the Mouseketeers, and she was a bit nervous as she prepared for her first day of class at a nearby junior high school. She hoped she could just magically slip back into the crowd and that the aura of celebrity would disappear. She wanted to make friends, good friends, intimate friends and, perhaps most importantly, non-show business friends.

Annette's first day back in public school was the worst kind of hell.

She had just walked onto the school grounds and was walking across the playground when she was suddenly surrounded by dozens of kids. They put their hands over their heads in a crude imitation of the Mickey Mouse ears and began chanting *The Mickey Mouse Club* theme song. The torment continued throughout the day. The kids and their taunts followed her to her classroom, to her locker and out onto the playground. Annette did her best to make friends and was initially good natured in response to their attacks on her. But nothing would stop their endless teasing. By the end of that first day, Annette was an emotional wreck. She ran home crying, the taunts of her schoolmates ringing in her ears.

Annette tearfully told her mother that she did not want to go back to the school. But her mother insisted that she go back the next day and tough it out. Virginia was torn by her decision. She and her husband had encouraged their daughter to be different. Now she was forcing her daughter to be like everybody else and, truth be known, she was not sure her sensitive, vulnerable Annette was up to the task.

Annette would go back to the school two more times. But the harassment was relentless. Finally the school's principal called Virginia and told her that her daughter's attempt at fitting in was not working out. and that it would be in her best educational and emotional interest if she would enroll her in the Hollywood Professional School for child actors.

It was a pivotal moment in the life of Annette Funicello. At age 12 she had bucked the odds and ended up a star. But her attempt at just fitting in and being a normal little girl had ended in total, abject failure.

CHAPTER FIVE

FRONT AND CENTER

Annette had learned a hard lesson. For better or worse, she would not be comfortable in an educational setting that did not include her peers in the entertainment industry. Among fellow child actors in the Hollywood Professional School, she was in her element as a student during her hiatus from *The Mickey Mouse Club*.

Easily one of the high points of the first season of *The Mickey Mouse Club* was the serial *Spin and Marty*, a very boy-friendly, light-hearted western themed adventure series centered around the title characters and the fictional Triple R summer camp ranch. The pre-teen male viewers ate *Spin and Marty* up and could not wait for more.

Annette liked the show and, in particular, the serial's co-star Tim Considine, who, she reportedly, expressed a strong liking for during the first season of the show. But she sensed that *Spin and Marty* was very much a boy's fantasy that did not have room for girls.

Considine, in conversation with *Animation*

Magazine, would recall that he did sense that Annette did seem to have a crush on him during the *Spin and Marty* days. But that he was uncomfortable with a thirteen-year-old girl following him around (he was fifteen at the time). "When I first met her, she wasn't nearly as beautiful as she became later. But she was always attractive. She always had this attractive demeanor about her."

But Annette did not count on the fact that Walt Disney, going into the second season, was now set on using every opportunity to work Annette into every possible corner of *The Mickey Mouse Club* universe.

Annette's relationship with Disney was always good, but as his protégé turned 15 and was acting very much her mildly rebellious age, Disney would often scratch his head at the reality of his young star acting like any normal teenager. Like most teenagers, Annette was very conscious of her looks and would often question that they were not quite right. There were the days when she was convinced that she was going to be fired from the show because she was too tall. Then there was the phase where Annette decided to change her last name to Turner because it sounded more "American." Disney humored her on that subject and would ultimately talk her out of it. But one thing was certain...

Annette was getting older and the mouse ears were not fitting the same.

Shortly after the beginning of the second season in 1956, Virginia was sitting outside a soundstage when a director walked by and casually mentioned that he was doing a *Spin and Marty* follow up and that Annette was in it. Virginia did not believe him at first.

Annette Funicello

But then she saw the script.

The Further Adventures of Spin and Marty, directed by the same director who directed Annette in *Adventures in Dairyland*, was your basic love triangle with good friends falling out over the attention of Annette, a camper at the Circle H Ranch across the lake from the Triple R. The serial, which shot from July to September 1956, was a comfortable outing for Annette. The script played to the wholesome nature that she had cultivated on *The Mickey Mouse Club* and, at that point, only an average actress in many critics' eyes, she was more than up to the task of the role. Needless to say, this follow up which ran during the second season of *The Mickey Mouse Club*, was another big hit thanks, in no small part, to the inclusion of Annette and, by association, the hint of romance.

The show's second season continued like clockwork; the cast working easily within the by now well established 'theme' segments and song and dance numbers. Whether Annette's singing and dancing skills had improved was constantly a subject of conjecture. But one thing was certain. Under Disney's edict, Annette was literally everywhere on the show.

By the start of the third season in 1957, the reality began to intrude on the fantasy. The dollars and cents of putting out a daily one hour show and, reportedly, the constant disagreements between Disney and the network on which *The Mickey Mouse Club* aired over budgets and the amount of advertising that should be allowed was beginning to be a distraction behind the scenes. A distraction that would become public prior to the start of production of season three when it was announced that *The Mickey Mouse Club* would be cut back from an hour to a half hour. But for Annette and the rest of the cast, it was simply business as usual.

And for Annette, the first order of business would be a big part in the third *Spin and Marty* adventure, *The New Adventures of Spin and Marty*. This third installment, which was filmed between July and September 1957, was less of a boys' western adventure than a non-stop series of music and dance numbers. Which was of some concern to the always insecure Annette. But given the nature of the storyline, which had seemed largely written to showcase Annette's talents in those areas, Annette continued to be adequate to the task at hand.

Annette had barely wrapped up the latest *Spin and Marty* serial when she was informed that she was about to star in her first full blown *Mickey Mouse Club* adventure, appropriately entitled *Annette*. Typical of Disney's traditional and, to many, old fashioned approach to creating children's television, *Annette* told the story of a country girl who comes to live with a big city family and, through several comedic and heartwarming moments, copes with the cultural change as well as such challenges as being the new kid in school. Despite its reliance on chaste romance, malt shops and cool kids wearing charm bracelets, Annette would always defend the show as having real messages and some depth to the storyline.

"*Annette*, whose title song "Annette" was written by Mouseketeer Jimmie Dodd, also became a platform for a tentative step for Annette in the direction of a singing career. During a hayride scene in one episode, Annette breaks into the song "How Will I Know My

Annette Funicello

Love." Annette at that point did not consider herself much of a singer. And had lobbied to just lip synch to another singer's voice. But Disney insisted that she sing it herself. Reluctantly Annette agreed.

Walt Disney broke the news to his Mouseketeers late in 1957. *The Mickey Mouse Club* had been cancelled by the network and that they would only be shooting the show for another three months. Annette was in shock.

The Mickey Mouse Club had come to be a second home for her. Walt Disney had been like a surrogate father. Annette was sad, confused and frightened about her prospects for the future once *The Mickey Mouse Club* was no more. But for the next three months there was still work to do.

The terms of the cancellation were that a fourth and final season, made up of original segments and a mixture of reruns from the previous two seasons would run from 1958 to 1959. Which ironically made Annette's first true starring role in *Annette* the "must see" element of the show that was just playing out the string.

Annette began airing in February 1958 and the song "How Will I Know My Love" was not the young girl's finest hour. Her fears that she could not carry a tune in a bucket were confirmed. But Disney had had a feeling about the song during the filming of the series and took every opportunity to insert Annette singing the song into an episode's storyline. Consequently nobody was more surprised than Annette and, Disney, when the day after the hayride episode aired, the Disney Studio telephone lines were burning up with the question of where could they buy the record?

Marc Shapiro

The next day, Annette was called into Disney's office. Where she was shocked to find out that her mentor was signing her to a recording contract. Once she recovered her composure, Annette insisted that she was not a singer and could not sing. But Disney insisted that she could and, based on his track record thus far, Annette could not argue with his vision and imagination.

Plus she was still under contract to Disney and the reality was that she had no choice but to become a recording artist.

But Annette would later in a Star.com story recall that she went into the recording aspect of her career like the proverbial deer caught in the headlights. "I remember being frightened every time I went into a recording studio."

Disney was looking to strike while the iron was hot. So Annette's signature was barely dry on a recording contract when she was in the studio with veteran musician/producer/arranger Tutti Camarata who had worked with such legendary singers as Billie Holiday, Frank Sinatra and Ella Fitzgerald. It did not take long for him to realize that Annette was not a great singer and to realize that this was a way to get more mileage out of the Mouseketeer star while she was still under contract to the studio.

But Camarata was quick to put the best possible face on the situation. He could see that Annette was extremely uncomfortable with her limitations as a singer but. through a mixture of humor, simple direction and a whole lot of patience, he managed to guide Annette through a workmanlike recording session that produced the projected single "How Will I

Know My Love?", a cover of the classic "Ma, He's Making Eyes At Me" and a handful of essentially B sides that included "I Can't Do The Sum," "Just A Whisper Away," "Happy Glow" and "That Crazy Place From Outer Space."

Camarata had turned in a passable series of recordings and had used all the studio trickery he could muster to punch up Annette's vocals. Annette was not naive. While recording had been a new and different experience, her opinion of her talents had not wavered.

In her mind, she was not a singer.

CHAPTER SIX

NOW IT'S TIME TO SAY GOODBYE

Which was why nobody was more shocked than Annette when "How Will I Know My Love?" was released midway through 1958, the single sold well over a hundred thousand copies right out the gate and would ultimately climb to a respectable No. 55 on the Cash Box charts.

Just like that Annette was a bonafide recording star. Which was just as well. Because by that time she could no longer call herself a Mouseketeer.

The last days of *The Mickey Mouse Club* were a stressful time for Annette and the rest of the cast. The big concern in hushed conversations between the soon to be ex-Mouseketeers and their parents was what would they do now? The prognosis for former child actors was not good and, for most, the likely scenario was that they would work very little or never again in their post- *Mickey Mouse Club* lives.

Annette was taking it particularly hard. She was not sleeping very well and would cry at the drop of a hat. She had come to know the Disney Studio as her home away from home. She was not looking forward

Annette Funicello

to that last day...

Which came on a Friday. After struggling through some final action segments in which everybody had to smile and be happy, the kids brought out their autograph books to sign. There was more crying and then...the Mouseketeers walked off the Disney lot for the very last time.

All except for Annette.

The Mouseketeer's original contract still had several years to run, and Disney, always the consummate businessman, still saw lucrative potential in his now teenage protégé. And so, a few days before *The Mickey Mouse Club* was officially over, Annette and her mother were called into Disney's office where they were told that Annette would continue on in the Disney universe. Annette would essentially be a contract player, appearing in Disney film and television productions while continuing to make records. Annette was thrilled and, more importantly, feeling secure in the idea that she would continue to work for Disney.

Disney did not waste any time putting Annette to work. By August she was appearing in her first major motion picture, *The Shaggy Dog*, opposite legendary actor Fred MacMurray and a number of alumni of *The Mickey Mouse Club* that included Tim Considine and Kevin Corcoran. Although a relatively small role, the experience of working on *The Shaggy Dog* and then watching as it became a smash hit was priceless.

Annette's budding recording career was also being addressed at that point. Hoping to capitalize on the success of "How Will I Know My Love" and to move Annette away from ballads and into the exploding arena of pop and rock and roll. Tutti Camarata would continue to produce Annette but Disney wanted songwriting input from other sources. Which led to the chance encounter on the New Jersey turnpike with a song called "Tall Paul," written by the songwriting duo of Robert and Richard Sherman.

"A Disney assistant was driving along the New Jersey turnpike when he heard "Tall Paul" on the radio," remembered Richard Sherman. "It was the version of the song by, coincidentally, another former Mouseketeer, Judy Harriet, and it was not much of a hit. The assistant thought it would be a great piece of material for Annette. The assistant tracked us down and said, 'We want the song to record with Annette.' We said, 'Who is Annette?'"

After they discovered who Annette was, Disney mad a personal call to the songwriting brothers, requesting "Tall Paul" and a co-publishing deal was quickly hammered out. The brothers Sherman did not know Camarata or Annette and so, as a professional courtesy, stayed away from the initial recording sessions for "Tall Paul." One day they did walk into the studio and Camarata played the first takes of the song and, for the first time, Annette's voice. They were not pleased with what they heard.

"What we heard was this smash hit background and this wonderful backup group," recalled Richard, "and then we heard Annette; this little weak girl's voice, tweaking out and barely audible half the time. We asked Tutti, 'Is that the record?' Tutti said, 'Well, she doesn't have a strong voice. We told him that they could not put this out and that it was not a very good record. The music was overpowering her voice. We talked to Tutti for a bit and suggested some echoing and doubling studio techniques that would strengthen her voice."

Camarata told the brothers Sherman that Annette was very insecure about her voice as is, and that any attempts to fix the song with studio tricks would destroy her confidence.

"Tutti decided that the best way to deal with the issue was to not tell her what he was doing because she was so insecure," said Richard. "He decided to just tell her that he was trying something different on certain takes. She did not know he was using studio techniques to save the record. It was amazing when Annette heard the enhanced vocals. It was like she was a different human being. It gave her confidence."

Camarata was so happy with the revamped "Tall Paul" that he immediately requested more songs for a second session, something the Sherman brothers were happy to supply. That second session would result in the songs "Jo-Jo the Dog Faced Boy", "It Took Dreams", "Wild Willie" and "My Heart Became of Age". Over the years Annette would record a total of 35 Sherman Brothers' penned songs,

But it was not all work and no play for the now very teenage Annette. Shortly after turning 16, and being presented with the best possible present from Disney, a three-episode guest starring role in her favorite television series *Zorro*, Annette began showing an increased interest in boys and, while continuing to live according to a strict code of conduct laid down by her parents, she began to date.

Her first actual date, with a boy who umpired her brother's little league games, ended in an argument between father and daughter about Annette adhering to an 11 pm curfew. In coming years, she would watch boys she was seeing be driven away by her parents and, in one instance when Annette was seeing a Disney studio crew member on the sly, the Disney hierarchy threatened the employees' job if he did not stop sneaking Annette off the lot for rides on his motorcycle.

In her autobiography, Annette would insist that "I had never been a bad girl" in regards to her dating practices, but she hinted, with a sly wink, that "she had done nothing that she would be ashamed of."

Following her three-episode stint on *Zorro*, and a heavenly crush on the show's star, Guy Williams, Annette found herself the center of attention as the newly minted teen queen. The fan magazines of the day were falling all over themselves to do breathless but essentially innocent pictorial and feature interviews and, with her acting and singing career beginning to take off and reruns of *The Mickey Mouse Club* still airing on a regular basis, the audience for all things Annette was seemingly insatiable.

But at the end of the day, what readers of the fan magazines discovered was that Annette, away from the spotlight, still lived at home, did chores and homework and, for better or worse, came across as being perfectly normal.

While still presenting themselves as a normal blue collar working class family, and amid stories that the Funicello family had not become rich through the success of their daughter, Joseph and Virginia made one extravagant exception when Annette was finally old enough to drive. Rather than simply present her with a license, Joseph, on Christmas Day 1958, presented Annette with a 1957 Thunderbird Convertible, which was ultimately customized by no less a personage than car designer George Barris, who turned Annette's ride into a carpeted, candy apple-painted car.

But there was one catch. Despite being able to legally drive, Annette's parents forbade her to drive more than a few blocks away from their home. Because in Joseph and Virginia's eyes...

Annette was still their little girl.

CHAPTER SEVEN

TALL PAUL

"Tall Paul" had "safe" written all over it. A bubble gum sound that was more pop than rock. Simple lyrics over Annette's studio enhanced vocals. There was nothing remotely challenging or aggressive about it.

But it was right on target in terms of what was passing for radio-friendly and very vanilla popular music in early 1959. So it was not surprising that "Tall Paul" was everywhere you turned on the radio dial. Records were flying out of stores at an amazing clip. And when the dust settled, "Tall Paul" had become Annette's first Top 10 hit. And when her follow up single, "Jo-Jo the Dog Faced Boy" also crashed the coveted Billboard charts, it was all but official. Annette was now a singing star.

And Disney was quick to exploit this new phase of Annette's career. A literal boatload of singles would be released throughout 1959. Two full length albums, *Songs from Annette* and *Annette*, would also come out that year.

A whole new world had opened up to Annette. A

Annette Funicello

world that was miles away from *The Mickey Mouse Club*.

When it came to the reality of having to perform her hits live and/or lip syncing (a bit of a cheat employed by most of the popular music shows of the day), Annette was well served by her years of performing live at Disneyland and being front and center on *The Mickey Mouse Club*. To be sure, there was some nervousness. But once the music kicked in, Annette would invariably come across as comfortable and appealing in the spotlight.

Which was just as well because shortly after the release of "Tall Paul", Dick Clark and *American Bandstand* would come calling. Annette was in heaven. Growing up, nothing would get in the way of being in front of the television when *American Bandstand* came on in the afternoon. And whether in front of the TV screen or in her room spinning 45's, music had become a very important part of her world thanks, in large part, to Dick Clark.

Clark and Annette formed an immediate bond in the wake of her appearance, singing "Tall Paul" on *American Bandstand*, and over the next couple of years she would be invited back to *American Bandstand* on several occasions. Through her emergence as a pop music star, Annette also began rubbing shoulders with a different circle of friends, the slightly older and more worldly singing stars of the day that included the likes of Bobby Rydell, Connie Francis and Bobby Darin who, to a person, Annette found down to earth and encouraging. These were not *The Mickey Mouse Club* type of pre-teen experiences she had experienced in the past. She was now in with a much different crowd and was being considered a part of their group.

While still a teen, Annette was now emerging as an adult in many ways.

Her group of friends would be enlarged in an oh so special way later in 1959, when, while performing in front of 18,000 screaming fans at a Hollywood Bowl concert honoring Dick Clark, she made the acquaintance of the reigning singing star of the day Frankie Avalon. Annette had always had a mad crush on Frankie, and so she was a bit hesitant when they met. But what she discovered was a down to earth guy who did not let stardom get in the way of his kindness and sincerity. Annette had stars in her eyes and it was love at first sight. But not in the way one would expect.

For far from an immediate love connection, their meeting developed into something equally good: an immediate and binding friendship that was the result of similar status in the music industry and equally traditional morals and values. They would often be seen together in public following their meeting at The Hollywood Bowl and the public, who followed both of them in the constant barrage of teen magazine coverage, immediately assumed they were boyfriend-girlfriend.

Frankie would reveal years later that he was attracted to Annette from the beginning, but that he was also intent on not having romance get in the way of friendship. "It was always pretty innocent between Annette and I. Yeah, we held hands a little bit and we went to the movies a few times, but that was it."

But Frankie was the first to let *People* know that

Annette Funicello

Annette was nothing if not a very pretty girl. "You knew she was very attractive, very pretty and very voluptuous. But Annette never flaunted it."

Songwriter Richard Sherman, who had by this time become a member of Annette's inner circle, confirmed that "Annette did like Frankie. They were good buddies. But they weren't really dating."

Annette would acknowledge in her book that the perception of Frankie and her as a couple was perpetuated by design. "We weren't really dating in the true sense of the word. But we were together all the time, and for us it seemed to be easier to call it dating then to go into a lot of explanations when we were asked."

In the meantime, Disney continued to get Annette before the public in every possible way. Shortly after she completed her *Zorro* episodes, Annette would go before the cameras for two episodes of the western series *Elfego Baca* that would air on Disney's new anthology television series *Walt Disney Presents*. Disney would occasionally field offers from non-Disney Studio projects and, if he approved of the script and storyline, he would farm out Annette for those projects. One show that met those requirements was *Make Room for Daddy*, the family- friendly series starring Danny Thomas. Annette would wind up doing six episodes of that show with a multi-part storyline in which Annette, playing a student visiting from Italy, attempted to fit in in America with the expected comedic results.

But these days, when she was not working, she could usually be found around Frankie.

And being around Frankie, it was inevitable that

Annette would eventually meet his manager, Jack Gilardi. Although informally involved with Frankie, the young girl immediately developed a crush on the much older man. She admired his sophistication, but the infatuation was tempered by the fact she had heard stories around town that Jack, who had one time had dated superstar actress Ann-Margret, was a slick, smooth operator and a wild swinger. Plus the feelings by Jack toward Annette were nothing more serious than him thinking of her as a cute little girl.

A cute little girl who, given the short term nature of most teenage romances, had already shifted her romantic allegiances from Frankie to another up and coming rocker, Fabian. Going against her own image, Annette became enamored of the gruff-voiced, somewhat dangerous appearing rocker. She would meet Fabian during a Chicago concert appearance later in 1959, when the pair was part of a rock and roll show. It was little more than backstage small talk but, in Annette's mind, there was chemistry.

The pair got together in Los Angeles where, as was the teen magazine custom at the time, they were set up on a "dream date" in which the couple would simulate a fun filled "date" at exotic locales and pose for often humorous pictures. While Annette knew this was more publicity than reality, she was taking this a lot more seriously and was over the moon at the possibility of spending the day with Fabian. But, as was the case with Frankie, her "date" with Fabian turned into just another long standing friendship.

Annette did not know it at the time but another pop star with a massive crush on her was already putting the wheels in motion to get together with her.

Annette Funicello

Paul Anka, like so many others, had admired Annette from afar. He was smitten by her beauty and innocence. Paul's infatuation with Annette did not come as a big surprise. Entertainers have always lead rather cloistered lifestyles in which the majority of people they interacted with were often other entertainers. It was not uncommon for performers to date and often marry those with whom they had the most in common.

"She was just the girl next door," recalled Paul in an Associated Press story. "She had that thing. She had the 'it' and there was just no stopping it."

Paul Anka wanted to meet Annette badly.

So he called his manager, Irvin Field, who knew a friend of Annette's parents. Joseph and Virginia were delighted to hear of Paul's interest in their daughter. After going through some arguably tough moments over their daughter's early choices in boys, Paul seemed, at least on the surface, like somebody they could live with.

And so it was soon arranged for Paul and Annette to meet for the first time at a Funicello family dinner. Annette was initially not overwhelmed with the young singer-songwriter. She fell back on the fact that while he seemed nice enough, Paul was no Frankie.

And with good reason.

Paul was not the typical pop star. Yes, he was handsome and charming. But he was also intense and serious beyond his years. He made it plain that teen stardom was only the first step in a long, serious career. With Frankie, the talk was rarely more serious than their latest records, an upcoming show or where to get a good pizza. Paul always seemed to want to talk about serious things, important things. Annette had become used to guys who simply wanted to hang out together and have fun. Paul's no nonsense attitude was, initially, not very appealing.

But Paul did have a lot of qualities that Annette appreciated. He was legitimate in his support of Annette and her hopes and dreams. Many nights they would spend hours on the telephone when she would tell him things she had never told anyone else. Everything she said was seemingly important to him, and he always had a knack for turning her feelings of insecurity into pep talks that would never fail to renew her confidence. To Annette's way of thinking, Paul Anka was very much a younger version of Walt Disney. Eventually their friendship, the fact that he was unlike any boy she had ever met and Paul's mature qualities succeeded in winning her over and their relationship, quite naturally, evolved into something more.

Annette took an all important step toward adulthood and the real world in the summer of 1959, when she was invited to join the traveling rock and roll show that was *Dick Clark's Caravan of Stars*. In those cost cutting early days of rock and roll, it had become a common practice for promoters to package a number of acts together and book them on cross-country bus tours that performed a seemingly endless string of one-nighters in high school gyms and concert halls throughout the United States. These were no frills affairs, with an uncomfortable 30-seat bus often serving as home to such legendary performers LaVern Baker, The Coasters, Freddy Cannon, Paul Anka and The Drifters.

Annette Funicello

Annette was excited when Clark made her the offer. Then she was apprehensive. Finally she was more than a little bit frightened. She was once again worried about having to sing live without the help of recording studio tricks. It would mean that her mother and she would be away from her father and brothers for six weeks.

But there was also the upside.

"I was almost 17 and I felt up for new challenges," she would write years later. "I felt the tour would bring me into the world and bring me out of my shell."

It also did not hurt her confidence that Paul was also booked on the tour.

Dick Clark, known on the rock tour circuit as a fair minded personality who would allow his performers a degree of personal freedom as long as their performance did not suffer and they did not miss the bus, made some unprecedented demands of the more adult members of the tour.

No drinking, no cursing and no messing around, sexually or otherwise, in front of Annette.

Consequently, the day Annette, her mother and, for a short period of time, her tutor boarded the *Caravan of Stars* bus, any hopes she had of fitting in with the other performers had already disappeared because of Clark's warning. The other performers, upset at having to clean up their act, would tend to avoid contact with Annette during the tour. Years later, Annette would confess that she sensed the resentment from the other performers but had basically been too shy to confront them about it.

From day one, Annette, her mother, Paul and the

tutor would make their way to the last seats in the back of the bus and would rarely mix more than casually with the other performers.

"We would come up to her and say 'Hi! How ya doing?,'" recalled Freddy Cannon who was on the *Caravan of Stars* tour as the result of a handful of chart topping rock hits like "Tallahassee Lassie" and "Palisades Park". "But there was very little communication between her and the rest of the performers. She and Paul would always go to the back of the bus right after the show and pretty much stay there."

Even with little in the way of contact, performers soon began to form their own opinions of the young 16-year-old who had her mother along for the ride. Cannon recalled immediately "Developing a crush on her like everybody else did. I mean she was so pretty, you couldn't help yourself."

Carl Gardner, lead singer of The Coasters, almost immediately pegged Annette for the lamb in a den of wolves. "You could tell that Annette was a girl who had been raised in such a way that she didn't know much about the messes in the world. She was the innocent who, you could tell, didn't know too much about life, especially boyfriends and things like that. I just considered her this very young girl. Beyond that, I don't know how I would describe her."

The *Caravan of Stars* tour kicked off in a suburb of New York where Annette confronted, for the very first time, singing in her real unsweetened voice, without lip syncing, in front of an audience of thousands. Backstage, Paul was attempting to comfort Annette moments before she was scheduled to go

Annette Funicello

onstage to sing "Tall Paul" and a handful of other songs. She was extremely nervous but, with Paul's calming influence, she went onstage to thunderous applause and launched into "Ma He's Making Eyes at Me". She was moving stiffly to the music and smiling nervously. Also backstage, Freddy Cannon could see that she was having a tough time.

"She was a bit shy and afraid at first," he speculated. "I had heard she was a bit unsure about her voice so I can only assume that she was afraid on stage."

Annette finished her set with the song "Tall Paul." She muttered "Thank you" into the microphone and literally ran from the stage. Backstage, Paul grabbed her as she ran off and immediately began to council her on her lack of performing presence. He reportedly told her that she could not simply end a set and run off stage. He patiently explained to her that after she finished her last song, she had to remain on stage until the applause died down, say, "Thank you, ladies and gentlemen," and then walk leisurely off stage.

Totally frustrated at that moment, Annette insisted that she could not do what Paul said. Paul would not take no for an answer and insisted that she could. Annette promised that she would try and then collapsed into Paul's arms. With Paul around, she was suddenly not so afraid.

Carl Gardner remembered watching the relationship between Paul and Annette with a slightly jaundiced eye. "I saw them as just a couple of entertainers getting together on the road and having a boyfriend-girlfriend thing. I also knew that it probably wouldn't last. The temptations were there and nobody could stay faithful for any length of time."

But as the towns and cities flew by in a blur of one-nighters and the other, more seasoned performers fell prey to the temptations of the road, Annette and Paul seemed to be defying the odds and cementing their relationship. In fact Annette, in later years, would look back on the *Caravan of Stars* tour as the moment when they fell hard for each other. Very hard.

Annette did not know it but Paul, in the unspoken rankings of performers on the *Caravan of Stars* tour, was considered the headliner. That, coupled with the fact that Paul's manager was also co-producing the tour, often found the couple being able to avoid long bus rides, going from show to show in limos and airplanes on many occasions. In later years, Annette would speculate about the preferential treatment but would never go into it beyond the fact that it was happening.

Freddy Cannon, with no animosity towards Annette, indicated that Paul was resented by the other performers. "It bothered me and it bothered a lot of other people. People resented the hell out of the fact that Paul thought he was better than everybody else. I don't think Annette felt that way. She was his girlfriend, so it was just expected that she would go with him."

Annette was warming to the idea of the *Caravan of Stars* tour and was having the time of her life. Her mother was homesick. She missed her husband and their two sons terribly. While she had been on extended trips in conjunction with Annette's professional appearances before, nothing in those experiences had prepared her for the monotony and sheer boredom of the *Caravan of Stars* tour. By contrast, Annette's problems with the tour seemed trivial. Because she had to keep up with her school work, a lot of her free time was not her own. And a bus seat was not the best place to try and get even a few hours sleep.

However, there was an upside. As the tour progressed, Annette was beginning to come out of her shell. Conversations with fellow performers became more frequent and she even made a real friend in Janet Vogel of the group The Skyliners. And while her stage performing style still left a lot to be desired and often included such mishaps as tripping over microphone wires and hitting herself in the head with the microphone, she was, by those observing her on tour, getting more comfortable in the spotlight.

But Annette was still the protected little girl and, whether by design or because of the efforts of those around her to insulate her, she seemed to have amazingly avoided contact with the realities of the world and the tour.

"I'm sure she knew what was going on," insisted The Coaster's Carl Gardner. "We were human beings and so we were having sex. Everybody was drinking two fifths of something every day, and we were stopping at a lot of places where the people would say, 'No, I'm not feeding niggers' or 'No nigger's going to swim in my pool!' I'm sure between Paul Anka and her mother, Annette was shielded from a lot of stuff. But what she did see had to be an eye-opening experience for her."

Likewise, Freddy Cannon felt she was shielded

from a lot. But not everything. "I know she had to see things like the groupies swarming us and the booze. She was a really sweet girl, and I'm sure a lot of what she experienced was a shock to her system."

Annette survived the *Caravan of Stars* tour largely on the plentiful emotional highs that seemed to come along even when the constant companionship of Paul was not enough to buoy her spirits. A four-day stint at the Michigan State Fair was highlighted by the surprise addition of Frankie Avalon to the bill. And when she was about to turn 17 on the road and away from family and friends, the Caravan performers, led of course by the careful planning of Paul, made just another night in a Texas armory come alive.

Annette had just finished "Tall Paul" and was about to go off stage when Bobby Rydell suddenly strolled on stage, singing "17 Candles" to the tune of The Crests' time honored classic "16 Candles". A big cake with the appropriate number of candles was wheeled out to wild cheers, applause and Annette in complete shock in the center of the stage.

But the best present she could possibly receive was still to come. At a signal, Joseph, Joey and Michael Funicello came running out and embraced Annette. In the audience, Virginia was so shocked that she had to be helped to the stage. The rest of the *Caravan of Stars* performers came out on stage to help Annette celebrate. It was a sign that Annette, after weeks on the road, had figuratively earned her wings and had become a real member of the rock and roll family.

The celebration would be short lived. Annette's brothers had to be back in school the following

Annette Funicello

Monday and so the next morning her father and the boys boarded a plane for the flight to Los Angeles. Joseph told his wife and daughter that he would call them as soon as they got home to let them know that they had arrived safely. But then there was no call on Monday, Virginia called the house. There was no answer. Mother and daughter were immediately thrown into a panic. They waited anxiously by the phone but, when no call was forthcoming in the next couple of hours, they began to fear the worst.

It was at that point that Paul stepped in. He made a series of telephone calls to determine what had happened to Joseph and the boys. Paul discovered that the plane Joseph and the kids had been on had an engine fire in mid-flight and had been forced to make an emergency landing. Happily, Virginia and Annette also found out that the plane had landed safely and that the passengers had been put on another flight and, subsequently, had reached Los Angeles without further problems.

Paul had come through again and Annette found herself even more deeply in love than she could have imagined as the *Caravan of Stars* tour concluded in the fall of 1959.

But unlike all great teen love songs, the romance of Paul and Annette would not last.

CHAPTER EIGHT

REALITY CHECK

Annette returned to the bosom of the Disney Studio after the completion of the *Caravan of Stars* tour. She was not the same girl who had left six weeks earlier.

People on the Disney lot were not sure what the difference in her was. There did seem to be a bit more confidence in her stride, a more sophisticated air in which she carried herself. Annette was not quite sure what was going on either. All she knew was that she felt a bit more mature and a bit more grown up.

After six weeks on the road, Annette would have been quite happy to do another television appearance or, perhaps, start another movie. But Walt Disney had other ideas.

The success of her early singles and her first album, *Annette*, indicated to Disney that there was a definite market for Annette as a bubblegum rock singer and he was keen on striking while the iron was hot. And so Annette, perhaps a bit grudgingly, returned to the recording studio, armed with a new set of songs from the Sherman brothers and the ever present studio magic of Tutti Camarata.

Richard Sherman recalled that Annette exhibited a renewed sense of confidence in the studio. Camarata did not have to exert quite as much of a guiding hand. Annette had proven to be a quick learner and had picked up the studio shorthand when it came to the recording process that was designed to enhance her voice. When it came time to double track her vocals, she knew exactly what to give the producer to make it work. And that attitude, recalled Sherman, made for a much less tense recording session.

"At that point, we were having a lot of laughs in the recording sessions. Occasionally we would have a song that Annette was not quite comfortable with and Tutti would say, 'Dick! Go out there and sing that song with her!' I would say things like, 'Annie, you know you're going to sound better than that.' She would hear that and just fall apart laughing. During those sessions she told me, 'You know I can't sing.' And I told her, 'Well, you're not going to dance on this record so you bloody well have to sing.'"

Sherman, in all candor, knew that "Annette was not blessed with a wonderful voice. She was no Julie Andrews. But she had personality and timing. She was Annette and that was just as important."

Annette emerged from those sessions with some potent, radio friendly hits in "First Name Initial" and "O Dio Mio" and embarked on the inevitable round of shows like *American Bandstand* where she found herself getting progressively more comfortable with the applause and the accolades. In that sense, the *Caravan of Stars* experience was already paying dividends.

But in the back of her mind, there was always the thought of getting back to Los Angeles and finding the time to be with Paul.

They had finally declared themselves a couple but, as they attempted to balance career and romance, Annette would admit that they were both often confused as to the degree of their love. Was it love or merely teen infatuation? And being teenagers, she reasoned, did they really know what love was?

The romance with Paul, based on his creative output during his time with Annette, was indeed very real. Two of his most endearing pop songs, "Puppy Love" and "Put Your Head on My Shoulder", were composed at the piano in the Funicello living room. The relationship, in the best '50s teen tradition, remained chaste, due in part to the fact that when Paul and Annette were together, Virginia was usually around as well. But Annette would recall that her parents were so fond of Paul and approved of their budding romance, they would often make concessions to the "chaperone" edict.

When Paul paid a visit during one of Annette's frequent road trips, Virginia would go into the bathroom and stayed there so the teens could have some alone time. During a drive from Toronto to New York, Annette's mother sat quietly in the backseat as Annette and Paul talked and kissed in the front seat.

That her parents approved of Paul and their relationship was more than Annette could have hoped for. Now if only the two young lovers' careers did not keep getting in the way. As their careers accelerated, the couple began to find themselves apart for longer periods of time. Cross-country telephone calls at three

Annette Funicello

in the morning were beginning to become more frequent. Paul would regularly send gifts and kind words from wherever he was in his travels. But the one gift she really craved, having Paul by her side, was becoming less and less of a reality.

That Annette was happy in her relationship with Paul had long been a subject of some discomfort by Disney and other image conscious higher ups at the studio. Paul would recall in later years the pressure that the studio put on Annette to end her relationship with him.

"The Disney crowd didn't want her to be involved at such a young age," he recalled in an Associated Press story. "We both had our professional careers at that point and they would continue to tell her it was just puppy love

Annette was growing and changing. And she knew that her feelings for Paul were the real thing.

The *Caravan of Stars* tour and her relationship with Paul had opened up her mind and heart to new emotions and possibilities and it was being reflected in heretofore behavior that was unlike Annette. She was becoming ever more conscious of her body and the changes it was going through. Annette continued to have moments of guilt over the real and imagined hardships her career had put on her family. It was during one of those moments that Annette approached Disney about seeking professional help.

"I asked Mr. Disney if I could go see a psychologist who could help me become more outgoing and self-confident," she remembered in her autobiography.

Disney's response was that her shyness was part

of her appeal and that going to a psychologist would change that. He asked Annette why she would want to change. Annette did not have an answer and let the whole issue drop. But despite having temporarily defused the situation, Disney could see the handwriting on the wall. The little girl was growing into a young woman.

A young woman who was steadfast in her opinions and knew the reality of where she stood in the entertainment food chain. In a conversation around the time she was finishing out her final contract with Disney and venturing into non-Disney projects, she acknowledged that she was quite happy with her professional lot in life.

"I enjoy wholesome comedies and that's just what I'm doing," she told an interviewer with Major Smolinski.com who dared broach the question of stereotyping. "I know a lot of people make fun of these pictures but those same people would like nothing better than to be in one of them. I'm not interested in doing a Broadway play. I've been told that makes me unique."

She was also quick to acknowledge that her time as an actress might well be coming to an end. "After my Disney contract expires, I might retire, get married and have a big family."

Annette definitely knew her own mind and things would never be the same.

One thing that had definitely changed was a growing sophistication by Annette and her parents about the business side of show business. Joseph and Virginia had taken another look at the contract signed by Annette and felt something was not right. They took their suspicions to an attorney. Attorney Harvey Grossman determined that, while Annette was being paid what appeared to be an equitable salary, an inordinate amount of revenues from the sales of her records was going straight to Disney without the benefits of royalties to Annette. Grossman advised the Funicello family to take Disney to court in an attempt to have the contract invalidated.

Annette and her parents were torn. Their lives had changed because of Annette's association with Disney, and they did not want to do anything that might result in his terminating her contract. But they finally reasoned that fair is fair, and the contract, as it stood, was anything but.

So they took a deep breath and hauled Walt Disney into court in December 1959. The trial was brief. Superior Court Judge Benjamin Landis weighed the evidence and denied Annette's claim. As the Funicello family filed out of court, there was real fear that Annette would soon be fired in retaliation.

But Disney was a smart man and a smarter business man. Why would he want to get rid of somebody who was making money for his company and, by association, for him? In Disney's mind the matter was over and forgotten.

But the relationship between Annette and Disney was now strained.

In the ensuing months, Disney would keep his young charge busy, and it was becoming a more common occurrence that the Funicello household was being disrupted by personal appearances. Things became particularly unpleasant when Annette was sent to New York City for a two week stand at the famed

Radio City Music Hall as part of the live show being held in conjunction with the new Disney film *Pollyanna*. Going would mean that Annette would not only miss her high school graduation but that both her mother and she would not be present at the first communion of her brother Michael. Annette cried her eyes out and, in an uncharacteristic example of teenage rebellion, called Disney and explained why she did not want to go.

The conversation was reportedly tense. Disney insisted that she had to go but also promised that she would have the greatest graduation anyone could ever have. The promise rang hollow to Annette who was resigned to the fact that she was under contract and had no choice but to go to New York.

Annette and her mother reluctantly boarded a plane for New York. Singing in Radio City Music Hall and watching as The Rockettes kicked up a storm should have been a highlight. But it was not easy for Annette to get excited when her mother was so obviously unhappy at the thought of missing Michael's communion.

Virginia's unhappiness was not lost on a sympathetic Disney New York representative who would risk being fired by arranging for Virginia to fly back to Los Angeles to be present at her son's special day and leaving Annette without her guardian for the weekend. The whirlwind trip, literally under the nose of Disney, proved just the emotional lift Virginia needed. For Annette, the idea of being away from her mother for two days would turn into a fun adventure.

When Virginia returned to New York on Monday morning, she was shocked to discover that, while she

Annette Funicello

was gone, Annette, who had never been allowed to wear much makeup, was waltzing around the hotel in big false eyelashes that had been supplied by The Rockettes. Virginia was not thrilled. But she could not help but smile at the image of Annette looking just a little bit more grown up.

Annette was happy for her mother but still continued to be blue as her graduation day grew nearer and, despite Disney's promise, there was no sign of any big surprise. And so it was that Annette, with heavy heart, did the first of two performances scheduled for that day. She was about to go back to her dressing room when she was stopped by the stage manager. An official looking man walked on stage. Annette was in shock as this representative from the New York Board of Education handed her a diploma as The Rockettes danced and sang "Happy Birthday" in the background. Tears streamed down her face as the packed house applauded and yelled. They were tears of happiness because, in Annette's mind..,.

Walt Disney had kept his promise.

It was inevitable that the personal relationship between Paul and Annette would result in the singer/songwriter writing a song for Annette to sing. But Paul, a bit leery of approaching Annette directly with the song, went to Tutti Camarata with his creation. Camarata was aware of their personal relationship and so was cautious as he said he'd take a look at Paul's offering. He liked the song so much that he went to Paul and suggested that he write an entire album of songs for Annette. Thus was born the album *Annette Sings Anka*, a true labor of love.

Annette barely had time to savor *Annette Sings*

Anka when Disney announced his idea for a series of three albums for the singer. The first two, *Hawaiiannette* and *Italiannette* allowed Annette the opportunity to stretch as a singer as she interpreted a mixture of ethnic pop ballads and rock songs.

"By that time we had become known as Annette's songwriters," recalled Richard Sherman. "We knew exactly what she wanted in terms of hooks and lyrics. Neither Annette or Mr. Disney ever objected to anything."

Early in 1960, Annette finally had another opportunity to act when she was given a role in *The Horsemasters*, a proposed two-hour *Walt Disney's Wonderful World of Color* film, which was to be filmed in England. It would be her first co-starring role opposite Disney pal Tommy Kirk, and her first truly dramatic part.

The Horsemasters would prove to be an eye-opening experience for Annette. But not in the way she expected.

For the first time in her life, she experienced the ugly, petty side of Hollywood. Married members of the cast and crew were openly carrying on sexual affairs. Her reputation as being Walt Disney's favorite did not carry much weight in England and so she was regularly dismissed, often to her face, as "the Disney girl" or "Disney's pet." Annette's feelings were constantly being hurt during the filming of *The Horsemasters*. It was to her credit that she reportedly acted professional at all times and did her best to ignore the insults.

Adding to her discomfort was her expected homesickness and, in the case of Virginia who was growing weary of the continued long separations from her family, depression. The sightseeing and very English ways that appealed to the traditional Funicello values helped salve their loneliness. But it would be the broadest smiles ever seen that registered on Annette and Virginia's faces when their plane touched down in Los Angeles, and they rushed to meet Joseph, Joey and Michael.

Annette returned to the studio and completed another album, *Dance Annette*, which, on the strength of such upbeat numbers as "Rock a Cha" and "The Rock and Roll Waltz", would quickly follow her previous albums onto the charts. Annette also attempted to put time into her relationship with Paul, who appeared to be losing steam because of the pressures of stardom and what she was discovering to be their polar opposite personalities.

By this time, Paul felt he was rapidly outgrowing the teen idol image and was already pointing toward a more mature career, which put him in conflict with Annette who seemed more than happy to play the teen star forever. Because they were so recognizable, they rarely went out on a public date, which bothered Annette who still held on to the fantasy of experiencing a normal teen age date with the boy next door. In fact Annette, when Paul was out of town, did occasionally date other boys. But it was never anything more than a platonic exercise that would, inevitably, end with her feeling guilty for having stepped out on Paul with another guy.

But those dates, coupled with the expected teen magazine stories declaring Annette in the middle of a teenage love triangle, raised a very jealous streak in

Paul whose growing moodiness would often result in heated arguments between the couple when they were together.

Annette would admit to dating behind Paul's back but that she still truly loved Paul. Too late, the damage already seemed to be done.

The arguments became a regular part of their deteriorating romance and would always end with Paul making sarcastic remarks that would leave Annette devastated and hurt. She still insisted that she loved him, but she could see that the love was beginning to disappear.

However, the emptiness of a declining love life was partially salved by her continuing workload. After a career of lightweight comedies and dramas, Annette was surprised when Disney gave his approval to her appearing in an episode of the television series *The Rebel*. In a chilling for its time storyline, Annette played the wife of a man who was killed by an Indian and in the storyline, it is indicated that she had been sexually assaulted by her husband's killer. Annette knew it was a powerful moment and, while uncomfortable with the storyline, pulled it off in what eyewitnesses to the filming reported as a first class performance.

Following her success in her first real adult acting job, Annette returned to a more comfortable fantasy with a series of promotional films for *Dance Annette* and happily returned to the set of *Zorro* for one final guest starring role before Disney came to her with her latest motion picture, the co-starring role of Mary Mary Quite Contrary opposite yet another of her teen heartthrobs, Tommy Sands, in *Babes In Toyland*.

Annette Funicello

Babes in Toyland, which also featured Ray Bolger, Ann Jillian and Kevin Corcoran, was a grand fantasy in the Mother Goose tradition that offered a simple love story, bigger than life characters and, for the time, revolutionary special effects while offering little in the way of a nod to the source material, the Victor Herbert operetta. But while an admittedly contrived concoction, *Babes in Toyland* was considered perfect for the very young Disney audience. As expected, Annette loved the fantasy and the opportunity the film would give her to sing and dance.

Sands, who for a time was being considered in many circles as the successor to Elvis Presley, had already been on the road at the time *The Mickey Mouse Club* was on the air, and so he had no idea what to expect when he met Annette for the first time on the Disney lot for a run through of the *Babes In Toyland* script.

"I had seen Annette a few times on *American Bandstand* but I wasn't really familiar with her at all," reflected Sands of that first meeting. "So, when I met her for the first time, she was a total surprise to me."

And a pleasant surprise at that.

"I took one look at her and thought 'Gee! This is a beautiful young lady!' She was very quiet and lady-like, and she was beautiful. I knew right away that it was going to be nice working with her."

Annette and Tommy went into a three-month rehearsal period in which she got to know the director, Jack Donohue, and grew very fond of her fellow actors, especially Tommy who she sensed was a terrific guy and somebody who would be easy to work with.

Tommy had a similar feeling about Annette. But he knew that romance or even the hint of something more than a professional relationship was out of the question.

"I was much older than Annette, and I was married (to Nancy Sinatra) at the time. Yes, we were very friendly, but there was definitely no romantic feeling. Besides, Annette was not the kind of girl who would ever find herself attracted to a married man."

Shortly before filming began on *Babes in Toyland*, Disney decided that Annette and Tommy were also a perfect match musically and brought them into the studio to record songs for the *Babes in Toyland* soundtrack album as well as the song "Let's Get Together" and the title song for the upcoming Disney movie *The Parent Trap*.

The chemistry in the studio, as it would be on the set of *Babes in Toyland*, was never less than cordial and friendly, despite the fact that Tommy readily admitted, "There was such a difference in our age and experience that we didn't really have a lot to talk about."

But the seemingly above-board relationship between Tommy and Annette during the recording sessions was not something that Tommy's wife was comfortable with. Nancy Sinatra, according to the gossip magazines of the day, was very jealous when it came to the affections of her husband and had, on more than one occasion, exhibited a big streak of jealousy. Annette did not know if it was true or not, but she knew that Tommy's wife was making her feel very uncomfortable.

On several occasions during those sessions, Annette would turn around to find Nancy staring at her very intently with an odd expression on her face. Worried that she might suspect that something was going on between Tommy and her, Annette approached Tommy and asked if Nancy had a problem with her.

Tommy was surprised at Annette's question but insisted that there was no problem and that Nancy, far from being jealous, liked her very much. A few days later a yellow rose arrived at the studio with a note from Nancy saying that she was sorry if her staring had offended Annette and that she was a big fan of hers.

Filming finally began midway through 1960 on the Disney lot. Unlike previous Disney projects, a total of four massive soundstages had been given over to *Babes in Toyland* to accommodate the special effects, the larger than life size sets and the large number of song and dance numbers that populated the film. The word around the lot was that Disney was taking a number of creative and financial risks with the film and so there was an undercurrent of pressure.

According to Tommy, however, you could not tell it from the very first day on the set. "Everybody was very relaxed. The director was telling a lot of jokes and everybody was laughing. Annette was not nervous. She was very cool and comfortable that first day."

And the reason was that, following the uncomfortable experience on *The Horsemasters*, Annette was feeling very much at ease being back in the confines of the Disney Studio. She was also quite happy that her father had rearranged his work schedule so that, for the first time, he could be a regular presence in her work life.

The next six months would be a blur of activity for Annette. She had turned 18 during the months leading up to *Babes in Toyland* and could now work normal adult hours, which translated into a lot of 14 and 16 hour days. She would go home exhausted and immediately collapse into bed; only to be awakened, seemingly minutes later, by her father, a steaming cup of coffee in his hand, telling her it was time to go to work.

Annette had welcomed the childlike quality of the *Babes in Toyland* script and was literally a little girl again as she put on costumes, danced to ballet and classically themed music and worked her way through a number of special effects sequences. But it was not only the fantasy elements that made *Babes in Toyland* such a memorable working experience for Annette.

Disney had been a regular fixture on the set during filming and, in her private moments, she reflected on the fact that he seemed to be getting older. It was then that she realized that she too had gotten older as well and that she was no longer a Mouseketeer, but rather a young woman, and that *Babes in Toyland* was, to a large extent, an end to those innocent years.

Which, among other things, meant that Annette would have to become more savvy and aggressive in dealing with the business side of show business. And so in December 1960, Annette and Disney were once again in court, battling over the same contract inequities as the year before. This time the judge saw things Annette's way and ordered a massive restructuring of her contract with Disney. Her salary was immediately raised to $500 a week and to $1,050 a week at the end of four years. She was also guaranteed 40 weeks of employment by Disney and was allowed the freedom to make personal appearances.

Outside the courtroom, Annette was mobbed by reporters. She seemed oblivious to the impact the trial would have on her career but did volunteer that she was going to buy her parents a new car and new clothes for herself with her increase in salary.

A true sign that Annette was growing up was the realization that her romance with Paul was in decline and that it was time to end it. "It was obvious that we were going in different directions," she would sadly admit in writing about her life. "We felt that we could remain friends, but we also finally faced the fact that there were some things that even true love could not overcome."

Not surprisingly, Annette was sad and depressed at the breakup. But she rebounded rather quickly and remained quietly upbeat about the prospects of someday loving again. In the meantime, Annette continued to be content with the trappings of pop stardom.

She still made occasional appearances on *American Bandstand* and other music television shows but, by 1962, she found that, because of the evolving nature of pop music, her latest records had not done well. But Annette was not worried. In fact she welcomed this sign that part of her life was behind her and was anxious, at age 20, to get on with her adult life. However, a sense of loyalty to Disney kept her securely in the Disney womb and her mentor was smart enough to see the dropping off of record sales and immediately redirected her in the direction of television.

In short order, Annette filmed two more *Wonderful World of Color* specials at the Disneyland theme park, *Disneyland After Dark* and The *Golden Horseshoe Review*. She was particularly happy with the latter special as it allowed her to indulge her passion for cowboy dress up and make believe. This period was easily one of the most comfortable in her post- *Mickey Mouse Club* career. The structure of both specials was very much in keeping with the old Mouseketeer approach of simple lines and simple production numbers and it would prove to be old home week as Annette reconnected with a lot of familiar faces from her old Mouseketeer days.

Following the completion of the two specials, it was off to Italy for Annette and her mother to film another special *Escapade in Florence* for the *Wonderful World of Color*.

The trip to Italy was a fun experience; made all the more so by the fact that Virginia got the idea to exchange their first class airline tickets for coach seats and to apply the balance toward tickets for Joseph, Joey and Michael to come over later and join them. For the very first time, the entire Funicello family was able to watch Annette work and, on the weekends, see Italy in a way that brought the Funicello family roots to life for Annette and her brothers.

Annette returned to the states and ushered in 1963 with a wonderful, traditional family New Year's Eve party. There was singing and dancing and ample amounts of Italian food. Annette was having a wonderful time.

But inside she was alone with some very important thoughts.

She would be 21 in a few months and was beginning to feel uncomfortable with the whole innocent teen image that Disney was continuing to perpetuate. She was still under contract to Disney and would continue to honor it and his wishes. But there were already hints along the Hollywood grapevine that more mature roles could be in the offing. For the first time, Annette was considering an outside agent.

She went to her good friend Frankie for advice. Frankie suggested that she talk to his agent, Jack Gilardi.

CHAPTER NINE

HIT THE BEACH

In Annette's eyes, Jack Gilardi was smooth and charming; qualities that did not necessarily translate into romantic interest. But Frankie had assured her that he was very good at what he did, and one need only look at how far Frankie had come in his career to see that he was good at his job. It also did not hurt that, in meetings with Annette's parents, he impressed Joseph and Virginia with his business acumen and, most importantly to them, his sincerity and belief in traditional values.

For Annette, Jack was part of a personal and emotional equation that had been with her all her life. He was not, at least that she could see, a wild swinger. He was conservative, a straight arrow and, perhaps most importantly, he was very much like her father.

And so, despite still being under contract to Disney and feeling an obligation to the man who had discovered her and given her a career, she signed on with Jack to secure her non-Disney-related work. How Disney felt about her doing this was never certain. If he was upset by Annette's decision he did not show it.

Annette Funicello

Public displays of anger, at least around Annette, had never been his style.

Jack took his newfound association with Annette seriously and was determined to expand her profile beyond the aura of Disney innocence. His instincts told him that there was a woman behind the carefully created Disney persona, and he was convinced that Annette should be playing more mature roles. Disney, per his contract agreement with Annette, continued to have script approval over all of her non-Disney projects but he was comfortable with Jack and saw the benefit of Annette stretching her wings.

Which was why he gave immediate approval for Annette's guest-starring roles in the television series *Wagon Train* and *Burke's Law* in which Annette proved she could indeed play believable and slightly more mature characters. But neither Annette nor Disney knew that fame of a different sort was just around the corner.

American International Pictures had emerged in the early '60s as the king of the low-budget exploitation film on the strength of such movies as *The Creature from the Haunted Sea*, *Dragstrip Girl* and *Terror from the Year 5000*. AIP made no bones about the level and quality of their movies. They were not making great art. The studio was making escapist entertainment that would feed primarily a young audience's need to be entertained and not have to think too much about what they were watching.

The company's bosses, Sam Arkoff and James Nicholson, were always casting about for a new hot topic to hang a film on and, in 1962, had stumbled upon the idea of sun, sand, surf and babes in bikinis that had resulted in a lighthearted script called *Beach Party*.

Beach Party was designed to be shot on a shoestring budget, and so actors with any big name recognition were out of the question. "We couldn't afford any young stars because of our budget," producer Arkoff said in his memoir *Flying through Hollywood by the Seat of My Pants*, "so we started looking for people we could afford." In casting about for talented unknowns, Arkoff noticed that Annette "had matured into a voluptuous young woman. She had great potential as a star."

It did not hurt AIP's chances that Jack Gilardi had been responsible for casting many of American International's films. Arkoff and Nicholson went to Jack with the *Beach Party* script and he was quick to suggest another one of his clients, Frankie Avalon, for the male lead.

Frankie saw the reality of the offer. The film was fairly simple stuff and, to his way of thinking, a little bit embarrassing. But he also knew that he was nowhere near the level of trained actor and that he was being offered the movie to attract teenagers. So he readily agreed to do the film.

Jack did not have to look too far down his client list before deciding to send the script over to Annette. The timing for Annette to stretch her wings seemed right.

Annette was in between Disney films and her recording career appeared to be foundering. A total of six singles and three albums were released in 1962 and none of them charted. The feeling around Hollywood was that Annette, after a couple of star-studded years, was in decline.

Everybody connected to *Beach Party* held their breath.

The film was a fairly chaste affair. The only stumbling block to Annette's involvement seemed to be the fact that girls would be frolicking on the beach in skimpy bikinis. Whether Disney would allow Annette to do likewise, and violate his own well managed image of her, was a question nobody could answer.

Disney and a whole team of lawyers went over the *Beach Party* script with a fine-tooth comb and found it to be good clean fun. However, as expected, the one thing that bothered Disney was the fact that the script indicated that the girls would be clad in bikinis. For Disney that was a definite deal breaker, and he immediately called Arkoff.

Arkoff would recall the conversation years later in his book. "Walt was real upset about the idea of Annette appearing in a bikini, and I had to keep reassuring him that I had no intention of putting her in a bikini. But Walt wasn't convinced and he started getting real upset about it. He told me, 'I've nurtured Annette's image for years, and she's still my little girl'."

Arkoff laughingly remembered biting his tongue at the "little girl" remark. Disney was already upset and he did not want to do anything to kill the deal. Finally, Arkoff said, "Annette is twenty years old. We're going to let her mature. Let her grow up." Disney was flustered, but he finally saw the light. Arkoff once again assured Disney that his precious little girl would not appear in a bikini and Disney agreed to show the script to Annette.

The next day, Disney walked up to Annette on the lot. Annette saw him coming, saw the script clinched tightly in his hand and knew something was up. Her immediate thought was that it could not be good because he looked so uncomfortable.

"I've read this," she remembered him stammering. "It's good, clean fun and I think you'll have a wonderful time doing it. But I do have a special little request."

Disney indicated, in his oh so fatherly way, that the girls in the film would be running around the beach in bikinis but that he wanted her to be different and to not expose her navel. Annette smiled. Unbeknownst to Disney, Annette had been wearing bikinis for quite some time away from the studio. But she held back that bit of information and agreed to his request. In later years, Annette would reflect on this incident as an example of how she felt Disney was always a little bit overprotective.

According to Arkoff, the legendary "bikini" issue was more a publicity gimmick than anything approaching reality. "Walt really never had anything to worry about. Even if American International Pictures hadn't been contractually obligated to keep Annette out of a revealing bikini, we wouldn't have put her in anything but a more conservative two-piece bathing suit. Because, to be perfectly honest, Annette just didn't have the figure to provocatively fill out a bikini."

Annette was in agreement with Disney that *Beach Party* would be a lot of fun to do. She liked the idea of the couple trying to be alone for a romantic weekend

Annette Funicello

and she saw the comic possibilities of something or someone always popping up to ruin their plans. Annette could also relate to the inevitable breakups and jealousies that ran through the storyline as something real. But most of all she was looking forward to her good buddy Frankie and she playing something other than just good friends. She also giggled at the film's subplot about an anthropologist coming down to the beach to study teenage mating rituals.

Frankie saw *Beach Party* as something a bit more subversive. "The characters weren't clichés. If you thought about it, the characters Annette and I were playing were not what you expected. Sure, on the surface, we were representing the chaste boy-girl relationship. But Frankie's one main objective is to get Annette in bed. I mean I saw that in the first scene in the script. He's taking her to his beach house so they can be alone. It amazes me that people thought they were innocent."

As the March 1963 start date drew closer, Annette did have some butterflies. This would be the first time she had ever worked on a non-Disney film. She would be around unfamiliar actors and crew people and a director she had never worked with before. Annette felt she could make friends with anyone. But, over the course of the lightning fast three week shooting schedule, she found that her reputation and the "no bikini" edict had quickly gotten around the set, and it would make for some uncomfortable moments.

Several times during the course of filming, Annette was approached by the director, William

Asher and the on-set producers who openly taunted her in an attempt to get her to wear something more revealing. Annette stood her ground on the matter, refusing to do what they wanted, and, while her determination never stopped the teasing, she gained confidence in her own mind for not giving in to pressure.

Her memories of the actual shoot were fairly succinct. Lots of driving in cars and dancing on the beach. And since March in Los Angeles could get pretty cold, especially during many of their early morning calls to the beach, she remembered being sprayed with water to simulate her coming out of the surf and shivering a lot. Shooting on the beach was often difficult and so, for the more dialogue intensive scenes, they would go to a nearby soundstage which had been filled with beach sand.

As legendary as her not wearing a bikini was in *Beach Party* lore was the question of her hair. "My hair never moved, it never got wet," she once laughed while recalling the anecdote in her autobiography, "and the reason was that it was not my real hair. The director felt that my naturally curly hair would not photograph well and so they made me wear a wig that they sprayed with hair spray."

But while *Beach Party* was short on reality, what the film did offer was the chance to work together with Frankie for an extended period of time and the chemistry remained both personally and professionally. It did not always happen this way but, in casting Annette and Frankie, American International created the ideal comedic tandem. Neither was what most would consider more than an average acting

Annette Funicello

talent at best. But in the context of the lightweight storyline and dialogue offered up by the film, they had emerged as a rough but nimble comedic duo.

From a professional point of view, *Beach Party* was teaching Annette some valuable lessons. With only three weeks to shoot the entire film, extra takes were often out of the question, and so she was forced to concentrate and focus like never before to get a scene right the first time. Used to the more leisurely schedule of Disney films, Annette, in years to come, when viewing *Beach Party*, would often wince and roll her eyes at one take scenes that, for better or worse, made it into the final cut of the film.

Annette barely had time to dump the sand out of her *Beach Party* shoes when Disney, sensing that time was running out on exploiting her innocent image and knowing full well that her contract would be up in less than two years, immediately rushed Annette into another film, *The Misadventures of Merlin Jones*. In typical Disney fashion, *Merlin Jones* was a chaste romantic comedy involving Annette's character, by this time wearing very thin as a believable high school girl, and her wacky scientist boyfriend (played by Tommy Kirk), who gets involved with hypnotism and mind reading.

Annette was slowly developing a good sense of what was quality material, and while she would never say it to Disney's face, there was a real sense of predictable and, with the cultural changes coming in the '60s, dated quality to the script. But Annette remained nothing if not loyal to Disney and, perhaps knowing that the clock was ticking down on the contract with him, was willing to go along with his films until the end.

Annette had soon gotten over the breakup with Paul and would occasionally date. But those dates never evolved into anything serious. In her own quiet, traditional way, Annette seemed quite pleased with "playing the field." Although love, marriage and happily ever after was always her goal, she did not seem in any rush to settle down.

Especially when Jack was doing everything he could to keep her busy. Annette would return to television in '63-'64 with guest star appearances in *Wagon Train* and *The Greatest Show on Earth*. These were minor credits to be sure but, in hindsight, they offered Annette the rare opportunity to do straight ahead dramatic roles and show producers that the Disney created wholesome stereotype was not all she was capable of as an actress.

But even as Annette worked hard to destroy one cliché, American International was working overtime to create another.

Beach Party would open to solid commercial success and, in the true AIP tradition of getting blood out of a turnip, the studio quickly set about creating a sequel. The template for *Muscle Beach Party* was now set in stone. Frankie and Annette, lots of girls in bikinis and lots of music courtesy of the hottest '60s groups of the day. Annette did not seem to have a problem hitting the beach again, even as she sensed that she was trading in one cliché for another. She wanted to work and have fun. And the beach party movies would fill both requirements.

During 1964, Annette always seemed to be at the beach as she quickly completed *Muscle Beach Party* and jumped immediately into its follow up *Bikini Beach* and its follow up, *Pajama Party*. The storylines were getting progressively dumber, but Annette was comfortable in an environment that gave her the opportunity to meet several legendary actors who were doing the beach movies as their careers declined and to be around some great musicians and music.

With the days now counting down to the end of her contract with Disney, Annette expected that there would be another job from Disney and so she was not surprised when she ended up co- starring, once again with Tommy Kirk, in a sequel to *The Misadventures of Merlin Jones* entitled *The Monkey's Uncle*. Annette was once again thrust into the role of the pure, long-suffering girlfriend. Again while fun to do, the whole concept seemed extremely dated. But an unexpected bonus came when Annette was asked to record the title song for the film. Written by her old friends the Sherman brothers, Annette was thrilled to discover that she would be recording the song with The Beach Boys.

The Monkey's Uncle would be the last film Annette would do for Disney. For Annette it was literally the end of an era. There was a sense of sadness and nostalgia as she watched her long standing contract with Disney expire. A door to a very important part of her life was about to close forever.

But another even more important one was about to open.

On the surface, Jack seemed the ideal. He was Italian. He was Catholic. And once she got past the show business slickness that was part and parcel of his professional life, Annette had discovered that he had very traditional, very family oriented values. It also did not hurt that her parents adored him.

That the professional relationship between Annette and Jack would suddenly turn into a love match in 1964 came as a surprise to many. The way Annette would explain it, in predictably fairy tale fashion, was one day they just looked into each other's eyes and knew they were in love. But if one took into account Annette's significant relationships with men, Jack seemed the logical love interest. Like her father Joseph and, to a different degree, Paul Anka, the men in Annette's life had been kindhearted and quietly forceful. They were encouraging and, yet, controlling in a nice way. And Annette would probably agree with the notion that she liked being taken care of and told what to do by the men in her life. And so, despite the fact that Jack was 12 years older and light years more worldly, he was exactly what Annette had always looked for in a life mate.

Despite the warnings that it was dangerous to mix business and romance, Annette and Jack seemed to work smoothly in their agent/client capacity and avoided business talk when it came to romance. Well into '64, it all seemed to be working.

In the space of two years, the whole Beach Party movie craze had seemed to have run its course. Although still profitable, the G-rated humor and outlandish storylines seemed to be growing old fast. But that would not stop American International and, by association Annette, from riding the wave out until the bitter end. In short order, Annette was top-lined in such bottom of the barrel quickies as *Beach Blanket Bingo* and *How to Stuff a Wild Bikini*. She officially put an end to her stint as a beach bunny with a cameo in the so bad it was good *Dr. Goldfoot and the Bikini Machine*.

Annette had now outlived two stereotypes; the pure innocent and the bubble headed beach babe. Sadly, the phone immediately stopped ringing. Annette's choices had been lucrative over the short term but had failed to impress anybody with her dramatic skills as an actress. She had been quite happy being a B movie star and did not seem to mind that, career-wise, she had seemingly painted herself into a corner. Why?

Because Annette was in love.

CHAPTER TEN

LOVE AND MARRIAGE

Jack asked Annette's father for his daughter's hand in marriage on Father's Day 1964. It was during one of the many family barbecues the Funicello clan regularly put on in their backyard and, in the past year, it was not surprising that Jack was there. At one point in the day, Jack and Joseph walked out by the pool. That was the moment when Jack asked Joseph for his daughter's hand in marriage. Joseph was shocked. Then he cried.

They were tears of happiness.

Annette would often laughingly recall that asking for her hand in marriage went a lot further than getting approval from her father, as she stated in a *St. Petersburg Times* article. "When my husband asked me to marry him, he first had to ask my dad and then he had to ask Mr. Disney. That's how close we were."

Annette had wanted a storybook wedding. The specially designed wedding gown would be right out of a fantasy. Her best friends, including Shelly Fabares and, of course, Frankie Avalon, would be there as bridesmaid and usher. Annette dreamed of the perfect wedding.

But there would be bumps in the road.

Annette and Jack had wanted a Valentine's Day wedding. But when Valentine's Day fell during the period of Lent, a schedule change was made. Drawing up her guest list would be bittersweet. What would be later determined to be the early onset of cancer would keep Walt Disney from attending and longtime Mouseketeer friend Jimmy Dodd had recently died.

And then there were the threats.

For some time, Annette had been receiving love letters from a soldier stationed in Germany. Annette had been getting letters like that since her Mouseketeer days, and normally ignored them. As was the custom she turned the letters over to Disney security. But with the official announcement of the wedding now front page news, the letters began to take on a more deranged threatening tone. In one instance a letter proposed marriage, stating that if he could not have Annette, nobody else would. With that Disney security moved to high alert.

Consequently on the day Annette and Jack tied the knot at Saint Cyril's Church, security people dressed in wedding finery were all over the grounds, albeit unobtrusively. Annette would often recall that she was concerned about her safety and that of her guests but had been determined to not let the concerns spoil her special day.

The wedding ceremony would ultimately turn out to be the dream Annette had hoped for; full of traditional religious moments, the bride being walked down the aisle by her father in grand manner and, finally, the simple yet quite moving ceremony that ended with Annette and Jack being pronounced man and wife. More than one attendee would describe the ceremony as a scene right out of a movie. Which is exactly what Annette had hoped for.

The reception at the Beverly Hilton Hotel was followed by a honeymoon in Mexico. The dream marriage hit an immediate bump in the road when Annette suffered an attack of homesickness and told Jack she wanted to go home. Ever the considerate husband, Jack suggested that a call home to Annette's parents would make her feel better. It only ended up making her feel worse, and it would result in the newlyweds' first fight and not speaking to each other for two days. Annette would later acknowledge that the fact that she had been sheltered all her life and had not been independent which had been the cause of the honeymoon meltdown.

"I suppose if I had traveled alone more, if I spent some time on my own before I married, it might have been different. But all I could think of was home."

The couple would eventually make up and by the time their plane touched down in Los Angeles, they were once again happy and in love. Annette's parents met them at the airport. After the expected hugs and kisses, Virginia took a step back, looked her daughter up and down and, without batting an eye, calmly said to Annette...

"Annette, you're pregnant."

Annette, Jack and Joseph were shocked and surprised at Virginia's comment, openly questioning how she could know such a thing. But Annette's mother insisted her daughter, just back from her honeymoon, was now with child. Annette returned to work, appearing in a strenuous song and dance number on the television music show *Hullaballo*. Shortly after that a doctor's examination proved Virginia right.

Three weeks after getting married, Annette was indeed pregnant.

Annette had always fantasized about the possibility of starting her family on her honeymoon. But she was definitely surprised when this fantasy became a reality. The fantasy would continue during Annette and Jack's early months together. Settled in their Beverly Hills home, Annette was constantly surrounded by her family as she dealt with the early onset of morning sickness, ate to her heart's content and contemplated the new life growing inside her.

Professionally there was some unfinished business. In the early months of her pregnancy, she had two films to complete. Being pregnant caused some slight changes in her wardrobe for *How to Stuff a Wild Bikini*. For that film she was now wearing non revealing oversized clothing. In *Dr. Goldfoot and the Bikini Machine*. It was more oversized clothing and an even more abbreviated cameo than had been previously intended.

Annette would often acknowledge that in the months leading up to the birth of her first child her life was constantly on the job training. While preparing to be a new mother, she was also hard at work, with the aid of her mother, learning the ins and outs of being a good wife to her husband. Annette seemed fine with traditional wife/homemaker duties and, subconsciously, was putting her professional life behind her and moving toward a total domestic one as wife and mother.

Gina Luree Gilardi was born on October 17, 1965. It was a joyous occasion with Disney characters, courtesy of Walt Disney, offering flowers and congratulations from Walt Disney. Her good friend Frankie was on hand. Annette was overcome with the joy and happiness of new motherhood.

Annette and Jack soon bought a home in Encino, California, and, while Jack continued the slick Hollywood operator during the day, he was always the kind, loving and attentive husband and father at home. Jack would never pressure Annette on the professional front and it was an unwritten rule that the new mother would only work when and where she wanted.

During the first year there would be occasional guest appearances on the likes of *The Ed Sullivan Show*. On those occasions, Annette was always secure in the knowledge that she had the best babysitters in the world in her mom and dad. And although she would occasionally get scripts, she was being picky. A true test of her struggles between career and motherhood would be the film *Fireball 500*.

With the beach movie cycle all but dead, American International had been casting around for another idea for a cycle of teen rebellion films. They decided that car racing movies was the way to go and, with *Fireball 500*, casting Annette, Frankie and Fabian seemed the ideal marketing ploy. Annette reluctantly agreed, primarily because it was a chance to reunite with old friends from the beach party days.

But emotionally it was a struggle.

Fireball 500 was filmed in and around Los Angeles which allowed for a leisurely Monday through Friday shooting schedule. The downside was

Annette Funicello

that Annette was constantly distracted. She knew her daughter was in safe hands but her motherly instinct was now at an all time high. She would race home at the end of each shooting day to be with Gina and would count the days until the weekend when she could just be Annette, wife and mother. Although she would do two more movies between '66 and '67, *Thunder Alley* and The Monkees' psychedelic romp, *Head*, emotionally Annette had finally had enough of the time away from her daughter While she would occasionally do a guest appearance on a TV show, such as the solid acting turn in an episode of the series *Hondo*, she had, for all intents and purposes, given up her professional life to be a stay at home mother.

Walt Disney's passing in 1966 would hit Annette very hard. He had been her second father for years, and although, at its core, it was a professional relationship, Annette was shocked and saddened at the passing of the man who had come to mean so much to her. In an emotional sense, things would never be completely the same. Because she would have one regret…

That she did not get to say goodbye.

During the late '60s, Annette was in a state of domestic bliss. She would make it plain that she was not interested in working anymore. But that did not keep filmmakers from knocking on Annette's door with offers that were nothing if not interesting. Annette's squeaky clean, innocent and, yes, virginal image had become so ingrained in the public's consciousness, that it was almost inevitable that progressive movie makers were tempted to take her to the dark side. Consequently there was a period where

Annette would receive scripts in which her character was a drunk, a drug addict or a prostitute. Annette was amazed at the attempts to get her to play against type but always turned them down. Those roles were simply not her.

Annette and Jack were thrilled to discover that she was once again pregnant midway through 1969. On February 10, 1970, Jack Gilardi Jr. was born. For Annette the fairytale life of wife and mother was continuing at a steady pace. She had literally become the perfect sitcom mother; fulfilled in stay at home chores, moving easily in non-show biz circles in school activities, and delighting in all the big and small moments of her children's life.

Her daughter Gina would recall in *In Style* that "She was always there for carpools, Hot Dog Day and the PTA."

But less than six years into their marriage, there was already signs of trouble.

Because Jack was a mover and shaker in Hollywood, it had always been a part of his job to mix and mingle socially. Before they were married, Annette would go to social events with Jack and do her best to fit in. But she was uncomfortable; knowing in her heart that she was a traditional values kind of girl rather than a member of Hollywood high society. But she loved Jack, and she knew it was important for his image that she be seen on his arm. There were also those times when Jack would host dinner parties at their home. Annette would fret about those parties for days prior and, while nobody could argue that she was not the perfect host, Annette would soon grow to dread those occasions.

Annette Funicello

With the arrival of Gina and Jack Jr., it was easy to avoid many of Jack's social obligations and, to his credit, Jack was in agreement that the welfare of their children came first. Consequently Jack would end up going to many Hollywood functions alone and, by association, he and Annette were spending a lot less time together. Annette had her children to occupy her days.

But her marriage to Jack was beginning to ring hollow.

Through the ups and downs, Annette could always count on Frankie to brighten her day with a visit or a telephone call. Short of being lovers, Annette and Frankie were that rare Hollywood pair who had managed to stay close friends. And as it would turn out, they would continue to work professionally in the '70s because the indelible image people continued to have of the couple from their Beach Party days refused to go away.

In 1973, Annette came out of retirement when the producers of the television series *Love American Style*, offered Frankie and Annette the chance to work together in a segment of the romantic-themed comedy series. For Annette, it proved a joyous come back, full of good clean fun and a large dose of nostalgia.

In the true spirit of that show, Annette soon found herself pregnant for a third time and, midway through 1974, a second son, Jason, was born. Jack was elated and remained the truly attentive and nurturing husband and father. But with Jack often called out of town on business, Annette's children, perhaps some speculated as an alternative to her disintegrating marriage, continued to be the center of her universe. Dealing with the squabbles, the PTA activities and Little League, Annette, along with her parents and a circle of friends that included very few celebrities and a healthy dose of regular people, got her through her day and she would often beam with pride at just how good a mother she was. She preached traditional values to her children and it seemed to be working because Annette's children were nothing if not well adjusted.

The chemistry between Annette and Frankie had been so good that, in 1976, when Frankie was offered a summer replacement television variety show entitled *Easy Does It... Starring Frankie Avalon*, Frankie was on the phone wanting to know if Annette was interested in being part of the regular cast. Annette immediately said yes to the show that would see her involved in song and dance numbers and comedy sketches; all very old fashioned and bordering on camp. Truth be known, Annette was feeling a bit housebound on occasion and did like the idea of working occasionally. Plus it was working with her best friend, Frankie. In the best possible sense, it made the summer go by fast.

Shortly after completing *Easy Does It...Starring Frankie Avalon*, Annette returned to the bosom of her family; quietly fulfilled at having worked and ready to settle into quiet times. Everything seemed fine...

Until the night the room started spinning.

"I was washing my face at the sink in the bathroom when suddenly the room grew dark and started spinning," recalled Annette in her memoir. "I heard bells, loud crashing bells. I had to cover my ears."

Annette's first instinct was to get back to the

Annette Funicello

bedroom and wake Jack. Suddenly she tripped and fell face first into their heavy, sharp pointed dresser. Annette would later recall that immediately after the impact, she slipped into unconsciousness. She did not remember how long she had been out but she remembered coming to, finding a frantic Jack standing over her, yelling, "Annette! Your eye is gone! What happened to your eye?"

Annette's hands instinctively went to her face. They touched mangled flesh and blood. Even in her semi-coherent state, Annette sensed that something horrible had happened to her face. Her worst fears were confirmed when she insisted Jack help her to the bathroom so she could see her face in the mirror. A deep cut ran from her forehead to the bottom of her cheek bone. Muscle and tissue were protruding from the cut.

Annette's only response was, "I'm going to be a monster. I'll never work again."

Jack rushed Annette to a nearby hospital. It was a surreal ride. Annette would later admit that she was feeling no pain at that moment. She was drifting in and out of coherence and it was a safe bet that she was going into shock. By the time Annette's parents arrived at the hospital, their daughter was on a table in the emergency room, being attended to by a doctor who succeeded in stopping the bleeding. A decision was then made to bring in a plastic surgeon to deal with the facial lacerations and damage and, while Annette recalled being aware of what the surgeon was doing and saying while being told that she had most certainly gone into shock.

One hundred and twenty five stitches were

inserted into Annette's face. At the end of the grueling procedure, everything was back where it should be. Physically Annette's scars would heal and she would be as good as new.

Mentally? That would be a whole other story.

CHAPTER ELEVEN

THROUGH SICKNESS AND IN HEALTH

Given the severity of her injuries, many were surprised that, six weeks later, Annette was strong enough to resume her normal routine. Which, in Annette's case, meant driving. While driving on the freeway, Annette was startled when she looked back in her rear view mirror and everything was black. She managed to pull the car over to the shoulder and stopped.

And sat frightened as cars whizzed past.

After a few moments she realized that her other eye was fine and cautiously drove off the freeway and managed to make it home. She immediately consulted a neurologist told her that the blindness was most likely a side effect of the fall and that it would most likely pass. Eventually her vision in the eye did return. But the incident, coupled with growing concern about what had caused the fall in the first place, left Annette in a state of psychological unease. There were moments of depression in which she felt vulnerable both physically and emotionally. She was now anxious about the future. Annette's life time of fantasy had suddenly been yanked out from under her and, in its place, was a dose of harsh reality.

Annette was afraid.

But the fear, to a large extent, would go away as she returned to a happier realm of wife and mother. By 1978, she was also beginning to work again, albeit infrequently and nothing that would ultimately stretch her as an actress. Her first post incident job would be a guest-starring role on the television series *Fantasy Island*. It was at that point that old friend Dick Clark approached Frankie and Annette about a project neither could say yes to fast enough.

Frankie & Annette, the Second Time Around would reunite the *Beach Party* couple years later with Frankie as a failed singer and Annette as a now widowed house mother at a Malibu beach campus. The hour-long pilot would consist of jokes and the kind of sophomoric hijinx that made the beach films so popular. The premise would also play with the constant attempts of Frankie to get Annette to be interested in him again.

The one-hour pilot episode would be a joy to make, bringing back fond memories of "the good old days" for Annette and reinforcing everything she loved about her friendship with Frankie. Unfortunately, despite the clout of Dick Clark behind the project, the television networks uniformly turned thumbs down on the show, and it would die at the pilot stage.

But while television did not seem interested in reliving the past, Annette's newly christened image as Middle American housewife and mother was definitely of interest in the corporate community. In 1979, Annette was approached by Skippy Peanut

Annette Funicello

Butter to do a series of commercials extolling the virtues of the already classic bread spread. After years of being the pop culture personification of everything youthful, Annette would recall getting a particular kick out of playing a mom.

In 1980, Annette would get one more opportunity to go back in time to her beloved Mouseketeer days when *The Mouseketeer Reunion*, a special conceived to commemorate the 25th anniversary of *The Mickey Mouse Club*, was created.

The show, which would be a fun loving look back at clips from the old show with a modern day update of the classic song and dance numbers by 38 now-grown members of the Mouseketeer cast, caused some mixed emotions. Annette had kept in touch with many of her Mouseketeer buddies over the years and was looking forward to reuniting with them. But she was also good naturedly concerned about whether the years had been kind to their old bones and wondered if they could still move like they did back in the day.

As it turned out *The Mouseketeer Reunion* was a rousing success, and Annette, in the coming years, would often acknowledge how she was grateful for the opportunity that show gave her to relive her childhood.

It would be the last bright spot in Annette's life for a number of years.

Not long after *The Mouseketeer Reunion*, Annette gathered her children around her and broke the news that their daddy and she were going to separate. Annette would painfully recall the moment in her book. "I told them 'Daddy and I have not been getting along lately. So he is going to go away for a while."

CHAPTER TWELVE

ALONE

It was the age-old story. Jack and Annette had simply grown apart. And there was really nobody to blame. Jack was into being out and about and being seen. He was consummate Hollywood. Annette wanted to be home all the time with her children.

Annette conceded that she had been quite sheltered and immature when it came to dealing with the realities of life. She had gone from her parents' home directly to her husband's home. Because that's what good Catholic girls did. Sadly, with age came the reality that when they hit the rough patch, Annette did not know how to get over the bumps and make the marriage work.

In filing for separation and, later, divorce, Annette was easily taking her bravest stand as an adult. There had never been a divorce in either Jack's or her family's history. And when she shared the news with a very small circle of family and friends, inevitably she was told that she and Jack should at least stay together until the last child was of legal age. Which, in the case of Jack and Annette, would have meant staying together another dozen years until their youngest, Jason, turned 18. But Annette wisely figured that their children would be more emotionally damaged if they continued to live together.

But in the wake of the separation and divorce, Annette made a huge point of keeping the situation a secret as long as possible, largely for the sake of the fantasy that had grown in people's minds about her, according to a conversation with *People*. "I didn't go public with it for a long time," she related. "I believed people wanted to think that nothing bad ever happened to Annette. I didn't want them to panic"

Annette and Jack's divorce would become final in 1981. But by that time, she had already gone through many of the rigors of being a suddenly single 40-year-old mother of three.

The divorce would be amicable. Once he had gotten over the shock of Annette's decision, Jack did not protest any legal elements of the divorce. In fact, he even offered to continue taking care of his ex-wife's household expenses by continuing to let their business manager pay her bills. But in a sudden rush of independence, Annette insisted that she would run the household and pay the bills.

Even though she did not have a clue how to do it.

"I had never once balanced a checkbook," she recalled in her autobiography. "I didn't understand how the mortgage worked or how or when to pay property taxes. Between my parents and Jack, I had never worried about money in my life."

Nor had she considered the idea of being 40 and reentering the dating scene. Annette claimed at the time that she had no interest in entering a new relationship and laughed off her mother's notion that her phone would be ringing off the hook when word got out that she was once again single. But she would acknowledge that during the first years following the divorce that, despite a full life that revolved around her children, there were those private moments when she was feeling very old and very alone.

Work would remain sporadic at best during Annette's post-divorce period. In 1981, she once again teamed with old friend Frankie for her first musical venture in years, duets with Frankie on the Christmas songs "We Can Make a Merry Christmas" and "A Night Before Christmas".

Over the years Annette and her family had become horse people. They owned and raced horses, more as a hobby than anything else, and had along the way made the acquaintance of a like-minded horse person Glen Holt. Glen, married at the time and with four children, was very friendly, offering to help out if they needed help with the horses. To Annette, he was a good friend and nothing more. As the years went by, they would see Glen less frequently.

Years later, Annette would describe Glen as the quintessential cowboy, a former police officer turned rancher and a true romantic. Twelve years older than Annette and seemingly steeped in traditional values, he seemed cut from the same cloth as Annette's father and, by degrees, Jack. Glen was the kind of man Annette would be interested in. If she were interested.

Post-divorce, Annette and her family had returned to their love of horse racing, frequenting the local tracks and taking her children for a behind the scenes look at the horses and the stables. On a particular visit,

Annette Funicello

Annette and her mother were sitting in their regular box when Glen walked over and said hello. Annette and Glen seemingly talked for hours, rekindling their friendship and talking about what had been going on in their lives. It was inevitable that Glen would let Annette know that he was now divorced.

Annette was well past the age when she fantasized about love at first sight. But she liked the idea that Glen might turn out to be more than a good friend. Neither was in a rush to make it anything more. In the beginning there would be dinners that included Annette's parents. It was the traditional Catholic-Italian courtship. During this time, Annette's parents gave their tacit approval of Glen. At that point, Annette and Glen began dating.

For Annette, love the second time around seemed to evolve quite easily and naturally. They discovered that they had the same values and morals, that they were interested in a quiet, easy, non-Hollywood lifestyle. They were both looking for the same things in life and in a relationship. It was not long before they fell in love.

Annette was over the moon about the new man in her life. The day to day realities she had been dealing with were often pushed aside by the fantasy of true love that was once again in her life. The future looked bright once again.

And it gave her the confidence in 1984 to take a creative chance to fulfill yet another fantasy.

It had been some years since Annette had sung publically, but she considered recording a new music album. She had always had dreams of recording a country music album. One day, with the

Marc Shapiro

encouragement of Glen, and the interest of a Nashville- based producer, she decided to do it.

Annette had no illusions that she would become the next Dolly Parton. The album, more a vanity project than anything else, was quite simply another fantasy she wanted to make a reality. The tone of the sessions was set early on the first day when Annette walked into the recording studio. She was greeted by a group of session musicians wearing Mouseketeer hats. The resulting album, titled simply *The Annette Funicello Country Album*, was a good time mixture of country standards, a handful of originals and, most significant, an original song written by Annette, an ode to her parents entitled "The Promised Land". While not a commercial success, *The Annette Funicello Country Album* would be a favorite among her fans and the song "The Promised Land" would get sporadic radio play.

Annette would continue to take jobs occasionally through 1985. Most notably was a role in the television movie *Lots of Luck*, about a family whose life changes after they win the lottery, opposite Martin Mull and Fred Willard, and a guest-starring role in the hit television sitcom *Growing Pains*.

But work would immediately take a backseat in her mind on Valentine's Day of that year when Glen proposed. Annette accepted.

Unlike her first wedding, Glen and Annette were in agreement that this second time around for both of them should be a simple affair; a modest ceremony, a limited number of guests and a small after-party at a local restaurant. But Annette insisted on one concession to the ongoing fantasy that had been the best times of her life…

She wanted Mickey Mouse to be in attendance. Easier said than done.

A new group had taken over the Disney properties, and it was their bottom line policy that Disney characters could no longer be loaned out for private occasions, not even her wedding. Annette was heartbroken. But a few days after she was turned down, the corporate higher ups had a change of heart and agreed that Mickey could make an appearance because Walt Disney would have most certainly wanted Mickey to be at her wedding.

Annette and Glen were married on May 3, 1986. The ceremony was a simple one in which the couple expressed their love for each other and extolled the virtues of how wonderful love the second time around could be. Glen recalled the happy moment in a *D23* article. "She was so happy after she got married. So was I."

There was a real sense of old fashioned sincerity as Annette and Glen recited their vows, especially on Glen's part, as he recalled in a conversation with *E! Online*. "When we got married, we promised we would take care of each other come hell or high water."

At an appointed hour, there was a knock on the door. Glen opened the door to find Mickey Mouse standing at the entrance way with a plate of cheese. Amid an outburst of happy laughter, the fantasy was now complete. And after Annette danced the traditional first dance with her new husband…

She danced the next dance with her lifelong friend…Mickey Mouse.

CHAPTER THIRTEEN

SECRETS

By 1987, Annette had entered the second phase of her life. She was madly and happily in love with a wonderful man. Her children were now in their teens and off to college and into the next phase of their lives. Annette seemed fulfilled in just about every possible way.

And then one day Frankie called out of the blue with a plan.

For years Frankie and Annette had talked nostalgically about the good old Beach Party days and how, in light of the fact that a whole new generation was experiencing the sixties in a whole new way, it might be fun to do an updated version of the old beach films. For a while, the talks seemed like wonderful pipe dreams.

But when Frankie called this time, he was talking a serious plan.

The concept for the proposed film, *Back to the Beach*, was quite simply Frankie and Annette twenty years later. The decades old question of if they would ever get together is answered. In broad strokes, they

Annette Funicello

get married, have children and deal with a much different world with an emphasis on irreverent humor and heartwarming looks back. Both agreed that *Back to the Beach* would be an upfront spoof, but the challenge was to fashion a script that would have audiences laughing with them and not at them.

Paramount Pictures eagerly agreed to distribute the film, whose $9 million proposed budget was light years bigger than the typical beach movie budgets of the sixties. Word spread quickly about the film and a stellar cast of newcomers, as well as a who's who of sixties stars like Connie Stevens, Ed "Kookie" Byrnes, Bob Denver and the surviving cast members of *Leave It to Beaver* (Barbara Billingsley, Jerry Mathers and Tony Dow) eagerly signed on to the film.

Pre-production on the film proceeded at a brisk pace, and it was not long before Annette was reading the *Back to the Beach* script for the first time. And that's when she noticed something was wrong.

The letters on the page were suddenly blurred and very small. Her initial concern was that this was the long delayed result of her accident years previous. But finally she chalked it up to a natural loss of eyesight due to old age and put it out of her mind. But a few weeks later, with her vision apparently getting worse, Annette went to her eye doctor. He prescribed reading glasses and while not a complete cure, her vision did seem to improve.

Annette put the incident behind her and concentrated on the upcoming filming of *Back to the Beach*. However, shortly after filming started, Annette began experiencing other mysterious physical issues. On several occasions she began feeling an odd tingling sensation in her feet. Once the production moved to the beach for outdoor shooting, Annette began to have issues with her balance, often teetering uneasily in the sand. Even moving from a sitting to standing position was beginning to affect Annette's equilibrium.

One of the first to notice her sudden difficulties was Frankie who, after helping her up on one occasion, joked that maybe she had had a bit too much to drink the night before. Annette deflected the issue with a smile but as filming progressed, Annette's balance issues continued, and she was suddenly concerned that the onset of old age or something even worse was happening to her.

But her drive remained surprisingly high in the face of these concerns and, shortly after the completion of *Back to the Beach*, she jumped at the chance to do a cameo appearance in the film *Troop Beverly Hills*. This would be Annette's last motion picture.

A couple of months after filming concluded, Annette once again began to experience blurred vision. Her eye doctor once again ordered stronger glasses. Her vision once again improved but, literally within weeks, she was having vision problems again. When she returned to her eye doctor for a third time in less than six months, he knew something was wrong. After some additional tests, her eye doctor strongly suggested that she see a neurologist.

Her neurologist did a preliminary examination and suggested that Annette have an MRI, a test designed to produce images of internal organs and tissues. By this time, Annette was truly torn emotionally. Part of her was in total fear mode;

thinking *tumor* and all manner of serious and potentially fatal scenarios. While the ever optimistic side was quietly confident that the test would find nothing wrong.

Following the completion of the MRI, Annette and Glen drove home in silence. There was not much either could say, except that in a few days they would most likely know the truth.

Several days later, with Glen and her mother at her side, Annette sat patiently in the neurologist's office. It went without saying that the wait of only a few moments seemed like an eternity. Finally the doctor came out and offered up the results of the test.

Annette had multiple sclerosis.

Shock and bewilderment were on the faces of Glen and Virginia. Annette was in a state of shock as well. Her doctor patiently explained what MS was, what caused it and what to expect as the disease progressed. Annette only half listened. Inside her mind she was focused on her future and what it would mean to her family and friends.

Not surprisingly, Glen immediately stepped forward with his promise of support. "When she got diagnosed, I promised her that I would take care of her, and I'll do everything I can," he told *The Bakersfield Californian.*

From the beginning Annette and Virginia agreed to postpone telling anybody about her condition and, in particular, her father who, she reasoned, would fall apart at the news. There would be time to tell him, as well as her brothers, later.

But her children were a whole other matter. It would be hard to hide it from them. They had to be told…and soon.

Annette prepared for that conversation by diligently reading up on everything that was available concerning MS. She became well versed in all the questions that would be asked about the disease and, more importantly, how to answer them. But when the time came, all the preparation in the world could not keep her children from expressing concern and no small amount of anxiety. But Annette had been insistent that her children were aware so that they, as well as she, would learn to live with it.

Not long after Annette's diagnosis, *Back to the Beach* was released. The reviews were mixed and the movie would be far from a box office smash. But those who saw it came away with praise for a film that had been true to its roots and intent. *Back to the Beach* was a love it or leave it film. And enough people had loved it that there was already talk of a follow up with Frankie leading the charge to get a sequel into production as soon as possible.

Annette wanted to do it. But as the months passed and the symptoms of MS began to appear on a fairly regular basis, she knew in her heart that another film would be too physically taxing. She was not ready to reveal to Frankie the news about her illness and so, when Frankie came around talking enthusiastically about the follow up, she feigned indifference and, to Frankie, an obvious disinterest in doing another film. Frankie was disappointed and, without Annette's participation, studio interest in another film would cool as well.

However, Frankie remained her loyal friend and, over the next year, would be a positive and regular presence in her life as Annette returned to a quiet, homebody life with Glen and the kids. That the symptoms of MS would regularly occur was unsettling at first but, eventually, Annette grew to take them for granted as just another added element of her ever evolving life experience.

For a number of years Frankie, when not involved with film or television work, had been making a very good living on the so called "oldies" concert circuit, singing his greatest hits alongside other stars of the sixties. One day in 1988, Annette received a phone call from Frankie wanting to know, in an offhanded manner, if she wanted to do a concert tour with him.

Annette was torn. Her basic dislike of travel and being away from home, as well as the specter of her MS flaring up unexpectedly, caused her some concern. But Annette was also thinking in terms of her mortality. In her mind, she reasoned, she might not even be able to consider performing live in another year. This offer from Frankie could quite easily be her last chance.

So she told Frankie she would do it.

Visions of her old *Caravan of Stars* days came flooding back when she happily discovered that Dick Clark would be setting up the tour. Annette still had not told Frankie about the MS. But it was very much on her mind when she laid down a limited set of stipulations to her once again performing live. She would do primarily weekend shows and would have to come home and rest every few days.

Annette was literally giddy as she jumped into rehearsals with Frankie for the show. The show would consist of solo segments, a series of duets and a medley of other performers' greatest hits. Annette was equally happy with the between song patter with the audience in which they would look back on old times and memories while talking about their families and their lives now. By fall 1989, the Annette and Frankie show was on the road with a series of warm up dates, beginning in Yakama, Washington.

The response from the audiences was immediate and overwhelmingly positive. Despite her concerns about how her illness might impact her performance, Annette surprised herself at how confident she was on stage. There would be moments when a particularly intricate dance move would cause Annette some concern and it was on those occasions that Frankie would, instinctively, hold her just a little bit tighter.

After a short break in March 1990, in which she participated in a special honoring the first anniversary of *The New Mickey Mouse Club*, Annette and Frankie returned once again to the road where they would continue, sporadically, to perform for the next year and a half. The tour wound down to a final show in Las Vegas in January 1991. By that time, the MS symptoms were becoming more pronounced and, because of that, she felt guilty about not letting Frankie know the truth.

A long conversation with Glen following the final show centered on whether Annette should tell Frankie. Glen was insistent that Frankie did not need to know. But Annette felt that, after all they had been through together on the tour, he had every right to know. Glen relented and told Annette to do what she felt was best.

They talked. Annette told Frankie about her condition. They had a good hug and a good cry. Now

Annette Funicello

it was time to tell the rest of her family. As expected, her brothers did not take the news real well. Which made the prospect of crossing the last person off her list all the more difficult...

It was time for Annette to tell her father.

Joseph was far from oblivious to the fact that there might be something wrong with his daughter. For some time he had sensed that Annette was not well and would occasionally inquire about her well-being. She had been able to put him off by saying she was tired or that an old dance injury was acting up. But fathers have a sixth sense when it comes to the welfare of their children and, after a time, it became evident to Annette that he did not believe her excuses. And so one day, shortly after the conclusion of the tour with Frankie, Annette sat her father down and told him the truth.

"I explained everything to him and why I had kept it a secret from him," she recalled in a passage from her book. "He seemed to take it pretty well. I later learned that once my father got home, he dropped the façade and withdrew into a silent sadness."

CHAPTER FOURTEEN

THE BIG REVEAL

Not long after she told her father about her illness, Annette would make one last sitcom appearance, alongside Frankie, in an episode of *Full House*.

Then, for all intents and purposes, she retired from show business for good.

The MS was steadily progressing and, most days, there would be some reminder that the disease was slowly but surely taking over. Despite the constant physical challenges, Annette seemed to be in a state of grace. Without the pressures of maintaining a career, she was now free to spend her days with family and friends and make memories that would last a lifetime.

Which did not mean she had gone into seclusion.

She and Glen would be spotted regularly at the nearby harness racing track and were not shy about being out in the public eye as a family. But for better or worse, Annette was still considered a celebrity of some note and thus was constantly under the watchful eye of the celebrity press.

And their salacious off-spring, the supermarket

tabloids.

The illness had progressed to the point where she was often unsteady on her feet or, occasionally, walked with a cane. Close friends would often comment on these and other symptoms, and Annette would usually fall back on a lie to throw people off the trail. That would usually satisfy people. But to the tabloids, it smelled like a story worth pursuing.

Early in 1992, Annette felt the tabloid noose tightening when word got back to her son from a friend who told him that he had seen her at a restaurant the previous night and that it looked like she had been drinking. Shortly after that incident, it seemed like Annette's neighborhood was suddenly under siege by the tabloid press. Word was getting back to her that reporters had been knocking on her neighbor's doors, inquiring about her health. Glen and her brother Joey also began getting calls regarding Annette. At the height of the frenzy, even her relatives back east in Utica were being questioned by the tabloids.

The tabloid assault reached a tipping point the day Annette answered the phone, only to be confronted by a polite but persistent reporter for one of the leading tabloids who offered her a large amount of money for the exclusive rights to the story regarding her health. Annette reportedly was so upset at the call and the offer that she was literally shaking as she declined the offer. The reporter hung up. Once she gained her composure, she realized one thing.

That a story would most likely be coming out in this tabloid in the next few days, with or without her cooperation, and that there was a good chance that the story would not be true. Annette was being forced to beat them to the punch. She was being forced to go public with her secret.

"I wanted to go public," she said, "and I wanted to beat the tabloids."

Annette turned to an old Disney friend, publicist Lorraine Santoli, for advice. Santoli suggested one exclusive interview with a national publication. She further offered that *USA Today* and longtime trusted reporter Tom Green would be the way to get her story out. Santoli called Green with the offer of an exclusive interview with Annette. Green was already well aware of all the tabloid reports and gossip swirling around her. His first question was, "Does Annette have AIDS?"

That Wednesday, two days before an alleged "true" story regarding Annette was due to be published in the tabloids, Green showed up at Annette's house. Annette told her story. The next day, *USA Today* ran a banner headline in their Life section.

"Funicello Fighting Multiple Sclerosis."

Annette bought a copy very early that morning. She read the story over and over several times. She was satisfied that the story revealed her secret the way she wanted it to. There was a sense of relief that it was all finally out in the open.

But like much of Annette's life experiences, there was also a moment of doubt. To a large extent, her announcement would get the tabloids off her back, but she understood that they would continue to pry. She did not want pity, but she sensed that a measure of that would follow her revelation. How would her family be treated by the outside world and, in her darkest moments, how would it affect them?

She would not have to wait long to find out.

That day would prove to be a rush of positive response from the famous and everyday people alike. Floral arrangements and notes of love and support came pouring in. Paul Anka, whom she had not talked to in years, called and they had a heartfelt conversation. Frankie also called to say that he and his wife would be there for her.

Annette was flushed with the good cheer and support, but there was also the inevitable question of whether she had done the right thing by going public. She had not gone public to cause undue attention on herself and her family, and she certainly did not want her revelation to turn into a three ring circus of publicity and press.

But the first time she went out in public after the story broke, she was happily surprised to discover that nobody was asking any questions.

At that point she knew she had done the right thing.

CHAPTER FIFTEEN

SEARCH FOR A CURE

Annette had never had a reason to be angry with Glen or Frankie. Until 1993, when those close to her saw an anger they never thought existed in Annette's world.

In the wake of her announcement, Annette would do selected interviews. During one such interview with Vicki Lawrence on her television talk show, Frankie, who was there for moral support, suddenly dropped a bombshell. He confessed to Annette, Vicki and the studio audience that, prior to their starting their concert tour, Glen had gone to Frankie, told him about her illness, and asked him to watch out for her.

"Frankie and Annette were about to embark on a national concert tour that had been booked before Annette was diagnosed," Glen recalled in a conversation with *D23*, a fan site sponsored by the Walt Disney Company. "I would be with her constantly on the tour, but the one place I could not be was on the stage when they were performing. I was afraid that if she got too close to the edge of the stage while performing, she might fall."

Annette Funicello

After the taping of the show, Annette angrily lashed out at Glen and Frankie. She felt betrayed and foolish by their actions. She most likely would have declined the tour with Frankie if she had known that he was going to be not only her co-star but her babysitter as well. And Glen? Part of her was amazed and saddened that he could go behind her back and, yes, lie to her. But when they explained that their actions were guided by love and concern, Annette softened, acknowledging that if the situation had been reversed with Glen, she most certainly would have done the same thing.

Glen and Frankie were forgiven.

Annette had decided that, in the wake of her announcement, she was not going to retire from life and let the MS take its course. From the outset, her stance was especially proactive when it came to helping promote research and understanding of her disease. In line with that, she founded *The Annette Funicello Research Fund for Neurological Diseases*. MS had become a cause and there was fervor in the way she was approaching this new challenge.

When she was able, Annette would do interviews. To her way of thinking, this was therapy of a kind in that it gave her a reason to think positive and to get up and face the day. But, perhaps, more importantly, she was carrying the sword in the fight for MS research and, someday, a cure. There was passion in her words during those interviews. This was not just another empty celebrity cause. Because nobody could argue that she did not know what she was talking about.

Because Annette was living it.

"I have great faith there is a reason God wanted

Marc Shapiro

me to have MS," she said in *The Bakersfield Californian*. "I think the reason is for me to help others and to raise funds."

Annette would do everything in her day to day life to help her remain as healthy as possible while waiting for what she was convinced was a cure on the horizon. She adopted a low fat diet that her doctor had recommended for MS patients. She gave up smoking which those around her had expressed concern about since before being diagnosed with MS. She adopted a balanced plan of exercise and rest. And she did her best to live a stress free life.

Along with the well wishes of others, there were the countless suggestions for a cure. And true to his promise, Glen would be diligent in sifting through them, discarding the questionable suggestions and researching those that seemed to hold out some hope.

Throughout the '90s, Annette's search for a cure resulted in a myriad of treatment programs. She attempted acupuncture and acupressure treatments, injections of steroids and vitamin B-12, and massive doses of vitamins and nutrients. At one point Annette was taking fifty pills daily to no avail and when another reported cure would have required her to take 180 pills a day, she said she was not interested.

The degree to which Glen would now need help came early in the '90s when live-in nurses were brought in to help with Annette's daily needs and challenges. But it was always Glen who spearheaded the constant search for any scrap of information that might lead to a cure for his wife. Glen read everything there was to read on the subject of MS. He viewed videos, and he took phone calls on an almost daily basis from doctors and people who knew people who had seen improvements in their loved ones through a specific, and often exotic, treatment.

And Annette was more than willing to subject herself to just about anything that promised a cure. In one instance, she endured surgery to implant electrodes in her brain to prevent body tremors. She willingly tried what was being touted as a miracle cure but, when she had an adverse reaction to the experimental drug, she ended up in the intensive care unit of a hospital for eight days. Inevitably there were meetings with doctors who promised miracle cures but insisted on secrecy that ultimately turned Annette off from proceeding. In one instance, Glen was in contact with a doctor in Canada who claimed he had a cure for MS. Glen flew to Canada, only to discover that the doctor was actually a restaurant owner and his "miracle cure" was a suitcase full of ordinary vitamins.

While Annette continued to wait for news of a cure she was certain would come, she began generating ideas to make money for MS research. First up was a line of Annette Funicello teddy bears. A line of perfume would follow shortly.

During the early '90s she also began to reap the accolades of being an American institution. In 1993, she was awarded with a coveted star on the Hollywood Walk of Fame. Within weeks of that honor, a retrospective collection CD of Annette's greatest musical hits, entitled *Annette: A Musical Reunion with the Girl Next Door*, was released to critical acclaim.

Over the years it had been suggested that Annette's life and career would make a terrific book. And now, with her life entering a new and final phase, she finally agreed that the time was right to tell her story. Unlike the majority of recent celebrity biographies, with their emphasis on sensationalism and scandal, *A Dream Is a Wish Your Heart Makes*, would be a love letter to her fans as she wrote about her life in nostalgic terms, not running from but not dwelling on the negative and challenging aspects of her life and career, and always couching her story in the most positive, hopeful and loving terms.

This kind of book would seem to be a natural with major publishers, the consensus being that Annette's name alone would be enough to secure a publishing deal. But what Annette would discover was that good and wholesome was not a major selling point with major publishers; several of whom would reject the manuscript on the grounds that it did not contain enough sensationalism. But Annette would not take no for an answer and eventually found a home for her story with Hyperion Books. *A Dream Is a Wish Your Heart Makes* would be published in 1994 to rave reviews and very good sales; proving the publishers who had turned it down initially were wrong.

Because people did, indeed, like a story that played to traditional values and hope.

Annette Funicello

CHAPTER SIXTEEN

THE GOOD FIGHT

By the time Annette had returned from the set of the movie *A Dream Is a Wish Your Heart Makes*, it was evident that MS was beginning to make aggressive inroads.

Her vision was getting progressively worse. She was beginning to have problems breathing. And although she was steadfast and insistent in trying to walk, now often with a cane, she had gradually come to realize that she would be spending most of her waking hours in a wheelchair. Annette looked upon this aspect of her illness with particular distain. With a cane, she felt she was walking and not hampered by her illness. But when forced to use the wheelchair, she reasoned that she truly had a disability. By degrees she was finding it difficult to talk. Annette would continue to be positive and would often exclaim that "she fully intended to fight."

Annette's courage and determination was contagious. In the public arena she gave people with MS who seemingly had no hope the courage to keep on. To her closest family and friends, it was a constant reminder that anything was possible and that, indeed, a cure might well be just around the corner.

But, as the late 90s turned to the early 2000s, Annette's resolve was weakening and her depression was palpable. "I'm human and sometimes I can't help but wonder 'why me?'" she said in *The National Enquirer*.

Annette literally dropped off the map by the new decade. She was rarely seen out in public and, except for those days when she and Glen would go up to his Bakersfield ranch for a change of scenery, she remained confined to her Los Angeles home.

However, on those days when she had the strength and resolve, she continued to be an advocate for MS research, and it was reported that all contributions to her organization had been used to fund as many as five medical laboratories that were engaged in ongoing MS research. In the meantime, Glen remained tireless in his research and investigation of even a hint of a cure. Sadly, more often than not, he was dealing with quacks, zealots and the just plain "out there" notions. He would laugh at the person who told him that he could cure Annette's illness with a complex series of magnets.

But he was quick to point out that if a viable cure involving magnets was found, he would be the first in line to consider it.

Annette's step-grandson, Cannan McDuffie was quick to point out, in *The Bakersfield Californian*, that actively courting non-traditional theories and cures was by design. "She and my granddad were interested in finding research that gave them hope and seemed to be ignored by the pharmaceutical industry."

Annette Funicello

But while they remained positive, Annette's illness had begun a serious assault on her body. By 2004, Annette had totally lost the ability to walk. Five years later, she would lose the ability to speak. But as the years went by and the ravages of MS on Annette continued, those around her continued to marvel at the confidence and positive attitude she would display, even during the darkest emotional days.

"It was painful to watch her struggle for so many years," related Cannan McDuffie. "She just never gave up. She just never complained. She was just the definition of strength."

Throughout the ordeal, Annette's friends would rally in her support. It went without saying that her children were always there. There were always notes and telephone calls of encouragement, from celebrity friends like Frankie and Shelly Fabares as well as everyday people. In those moments, those around Annette would see a glimmer in her eyes and the hint of a smile. Having people around whom she loved and who loved her seemed to make all the difference.

Annette lived in relative seclusion throughout the latter 2000s. Her husband and around the clock nurses were her constant companions. These years were particularly rough on Glen who, despite a nurse always present, rarely slept through the night. As her breathing gradually became more labored, she would often have trouble swallowing, and Glen would often awaken in the middle of the night to wipe the saliva from her mouth to prevent her from swallowing it and suffocating.

The drama and the tragedy would continue to unfold. In March 2011, Annette's Encino home unexpectedly caught fire. By the time firefighters arrived, the house was a total loss. Annette, Glen and a nurse were all rushed to a nearby hospital, suffering from smoke inhalation but were released shortly in good condition.

Glen related the particulars of the incident in a *D23* article. "It was about seven in the morning when one of the caregivers woke me up and told me that she smelled smoke. I ran out to the kitchen and heard a loud pop. The recreation room was filled with smoke. I got Annette out of bed and put her in the wheelchair and went down the hall to get out through the garage or front door. The smoke was thick and hot and heading right for us. I went out the patio door, lifted the wheelchair with Annette in it, and put Annette over the fence and into the neighbor's back yard."

A sad aside to the fire, as reported by *TMZ,* was that the neighbor subsequently sued Annette, claiming their property was contaminated by toxins from the fire.

Shortly after the fire, Annette and Glen relocated permanently to his ranch in Shafter, California, just outside of Bakersfield, where Annette and Glen hunkered down to enjoy the quiet cowboy life. Days would often be spent driving around the beauty and solitude of the ranch and its surrounding acres. Some nights they would stare serenely at the sunset. If they were up early enough, they would welcome in the first sunlight of the day. They were truly in love in the traditional, romantic sense. Every moment, big and small, was savored for all it was worth. Because, even though it went unspoken...

They both knew that Annette did not have much time left.

CHAPTER SEVENTEEN

A MIRACLE CURE?

But Annette continued to be hopeful despite her declining health. "When I wake up in the morning, I like to think this is the day I'm going to hear news about an MS cure," she reflected early in the '90s in *AMC Biography*.

Inevitably the news surrounding Annette's declining health became sensationalist tabloid fodder, with Glen constantly put in the position of denying the stories. One such situation occurred during the summer of 2012 when the tabloid press was reporting that Annette had lapsed into a coma.

"Those reports are absolutely false," Glen told *D23*. "She is happy and loved, and we make the most of every day. If she wants to go shopping, we do that. If not, we just go for a drive."

Sadly, the reality was that Annette was going downhill fast. But Glen would not give up. He continued to spend hours sifting through everything that was known about MS and any possible alternative therapy treatments and possible cures that were dismissed by mainstream medicine.

One day he found hope in a fan letter offering the suggestion that a new procedure might be of help.

Chronic cerebrospinal venous insufficiency (CCSVI) was a condition common in MS patients that had been discovered in research by Dr. Paulo Zamboni. His theory was that MS caused the gradual blockage of veins that prevented blood from draining from the brain to the spinal cord; thus returning the blood to the brain and causing many of the symptoms of the disease. Dr. Zamboni's research indicated that MS patients who had their veins opened by angioplasty or stents had, in many cases, shown marked and immediate improvement.

Glen was excited at having a possible cure that seemed to make sense appear out of the blue. But he had been down the road of cures so many times already that he could not be blamed for being more than a bit cautious. He immersed himself in reading up on everything that could be found on CCSVI and found that the results of Zamboni's research had been inconclusive. Some patients claimed a marked improvement after having the procedure done while others had shown no improvement at all.

Glen ran this new theory by Annette's longtime doctor, Dr. Jeffrey Salberg, in September 2012. "I told him (Glen) that it was something that I had not heard of," he said in a *CTV* news story. "But I explored more information, who the people were doing the procedure and their reputations. I started having a little bit more confidence in the idea that the procedure might be worth trying."

Annette and Glen decided that this new breakthrough might be her next best hope and so, in

October 2012, with Glen at her side, Annette underwent the CCSVI procedure.

"When they started the procedure, she immediately looked more alive," recalled Glen in a WT5.com story. "She was brighter than she was before. The glow in her face came in."

However, doctors were less confident. They assumed that Glen, to a large and understandable degree, was thinking with his heart rather than his head. The more cautious indicated that, most likely, too much damage had already been done by the MS to make all but, perhaps, the most minor improvements of little consequence.

But the joy and hope in Annette and Glen could not be dissuaded. They were convinced that Annette was making small improvements and that the CCSVI procedure had been the reason. Which was the main reason why, despite Annette having been out of the public eye for nearly 15 years, they willingly opened their doors to a request by *CTV* and their program WT5.com, to come down to Shafter and do a piece on Annette as she was today.

This was a daring and powerful experience. Nothing in Annette's world was hidden or soft peddled. Cameras rolled on Annette as she was bed ridden, being fed through a tube and clearly showing the ravages of the disease, both physically and emotionally. It was not a pretty sight but, believed Annette, Glen and those in her intimate circle, an important one. People had the fantasy image of Annette in their heads and hearts. They remembered The Mouseketeer and the Beach Party girl. This was now Annette's reality and no amount of wishing and hoping was going to change that.

During the WT5.com filming, Glen would go into great detail on how the CCSVI procedure had come into their lives, the seemingly miraculous result of Annette undergoing the procedure and how important it was to gather money and support for further research into the CCSVI and its possibilities to help other people suffering from this disease. After all he reasoned...

"This is what Annette would have wanted."

Throughout the rest of the year Annette and her family seemed buoyed by the results of the procedure. At their most optimistic, they took every eye blink and facial movement as a sign that Annette was improving. As always, doctors cautioned that it was too soon to make definite pronouncements regarding Annette and that an upcoming six month checkup would tell them much more.

In March 2013, Annette went for that all important checkup. Her family and her legions of fans had her in their thoughts and prayers. Shortly after the examination was completed, Dr. Salberg made his findings public in NewsMax.Health.com and *The Bakersfield Californian.*

"She seemed more responsive to my verbal conversation with her," he reported. "She made clear eye contact with me. She clearly was trying to respond affirmatively to yes and no questions.

"I haven't seen this degree of attentiveness by her in years."

Annette Funicello

EPILOGUE

DANCING IN HEAVEN

Annette was taken off life support on Monday morning, April 8, 2013. She passed peacefully at age seventy at Mercy Southwest Hospital with her family and dear friend Shelley Fabares at her bedside.

After 26 years of being in Annette's life, in the end Glen was too distraught and overcome with grief to make any public statements and left that chore to her children and extended family members. Unfortunately, one of the first comments would be to, once again, dispel yet another rumor.

What is known is that, in the days following Dr. Salberg's encouraging statement, Annette's condition went into a rapid decline. The immediate family and close circle of friends began to prepare for her last days. Friends were in and out of her hospital room with increasing frequency. In their own ways, they were preparing to say goodbye. But with a literal news blackout at hand, the tabloids, in those final days, ran wild with the rumor that Annette had lapsed into a coma. Cannan McDuffie, in the aftermath of her death, told *The Bakersfield Californian* that nothing could be further from the truth. "She fought this to the very end and has always been coherent," he said. "She was a prisoner in her own body. I feel like there was no way she could have made it this long without the attention and love of my granddad and the staff that was always on call to help her."

Her death made news all over the world. It was figuratively and literally the end of an era in Hollywood, one many observers indicated we would never see again. Which made the outpouring of condolence and sadness particularly heartfelt. Because the struggles and passing of Annette were tied to a different time and place. There was a real sense of loss due to the innocence that had marked her life. When most celebrities pass, there is always the old bromide that "they were taken too soon." In the case of Annette it rang painfully true.

People in her life, personally and professionally, expressed their sadness at her passing as well as their memories of her. Not surprisingly, Frankie was particularly saddened by her passing. "She really had a tough existence," he told the Associated Press. "This is like losing a family member. Annette never realized how beloved she was. When I would tell her that, she would say, 'Really?' She was so bashful about things like that. She was an amazing girl."

First husband Jack Gilardi also offered up his heartfelt feelings to CNN.com. "She was such an important part of my life and she blessed me with three beautiful children."

Annette's children would have the final, heartfelt final words on the passing of Annette Funicello when they issued an official statement. "My brothers and I were there at her bedside, holding her sweet hands when she left us. She is no longer suffering…Now she is dancing in heaven."

FILMOGRAPHY

MOTION PICTURES

The Shaggy Dog (1959) Disney.

Babes in Toyland (1961) Disney.

Beach Party (1963) American International.

The Misadventures of Merlin Jones (1964) Disney.

Muscle Beach Party (1964) American International.

Bikini Beach (1964) American International.

Pajama Party (1964) American International.

Beach Blanket Bingo (1965) American International.

The Monkey's Uncle (1965) Disney.

Ski Party (1965) American International.

How to Stuff a Wild Bikini (1965) American International.

Dr. Goldfoot and the Bikini Machine (1965) American International.

Fireball 500 (1966) American International.

Thunder Alley (1967) American International.

Head (1968) Columbia.

Back To the Beach (1987) Paramount.

Troop Beverly Hills (1989)

TELEVISION SERIES AND GUEST APPEARANCES

The Mickey Mouse Club (1955-59)

The Mickey Mouse Club Serials:

Adventure in Dairyland (1956)

The Further Adventures of Spin and Marty (1956)

The New Adventures of Spin and Marty (1957)

Annette (1958)

Elfego Baca (1959) in the episodes "Attorney At Law" and "The Griswald Murders"

*Zorro (*1959) in the episodes "Please Believe Me", "The Brooch" and "The Missing Father"

Make Room for Daddy (1959) in the episodes "Gina for President", "Gina's First Date", "Frankie Laine Sings for Gina" and "The Latin Lover"

Zorro (1961) in the episode "The Postponed Wedding"

The Horsemasters (1961)

Escapade in Florence (1962)

Disneyland After Dark (1962)

The Golden Horseshoe Review (1962)

Wagon Train (1963) in the episode "The Sam Pulaski Story"

Burke's Law (1963) in the episode "Who Killed the Kind Doctor?"

The Greatest Show on Earth (1964) in the episode "Rosetta"

Burke's Law (1965) in the episode "Who Killed the Strangler?"

Hondo (1967) in the episode "The Apache Trail"

Love American Style (1971) in the episode "Love and the Tuba"

The John Byner Comedy Hour (1972)

The Mouse Factory (1973) in the episode "A Salute to Mickey Mouse Cartoons"

The Mouse Factory (1974) in the episode "Pablo the Cold Blooded Penguin"

The New Mickey Mouse Club (1977)

The Love Boat (1978) in the episode "Never Fall in Love Again"

Frankie and Annette: The Second Time Around (1978)

Fantasy Island (1979) in the episode "The Strangler"

The Mickey Mouse Club Reunion (1980)

Fantasy Island (1980) in the episode "Mary Ann and Miss Sophisticate"

Fantasy Island (1981) in the episode "The Unkillable"

The Love Boat (1982) in the episode "N.Y.A.C."

Lots of Luck (1985)

Growing Pains (1986) in the episode "The Chaperones"

DISCOGRAPHY

Albums

Songs from Annette (1959) Mickey Mouse

*Annette (*1959) Buena Vista

Annette Sings Anka (1960) Buena Vista

Hawaiianette (1960) Buena Vista

Italianette (1960) Buena Vista

Dance Annette (1961) Buena Vista

The Parent Trap (soundtrack) (1961) Buena Vista

Babes in Toyland (soundtrack) (1961) Buena Vista

The Story of My Teens (1962) Buena Vista

Teen Street (1962) Buena Vista

Muscle Beach Party (1963) Buena Vista

Annette's Beach Party (1963) Buena Vista

Annette on Campus (1964) Buena Vista

Annette at Bikini Beach (1964) Buena Vista

Annette's Pajama Party (1964) Buena Vista

Annette Sings Golden Surfin' Hits (1964) Buena Vista

Something Borrowed, Something Blue (1964) Buena Vista

Annette and Hayley (1964) Buena Vista

Annette Funicello (1972) Buena Vista

Back to the Beach (soundtrack) (1987) Columbia

A Dream Is Just a Wish Your Heart Makes (soundtrack) (1995) Time Warner

Charted Albums

Annette Sings Anka (1960) Billboard 21. Cashbox 23

Hawaiianette (1960) Billboard 38. Cashbox 50.

Annette's Beach Party (1963) Billboard 39. Cashbox 36.

Muscle Beach Party (1964) Cashbox 72.

Singles

"I Can't Do the Sum"/"Just A Whisper Away" (1957) Disneyland

"How Will I Know My Love?"/"Annette" (by Jimmy Dodd) (1957) Disneyland

"Happy Glow"/"That Crazy Place from Outer Space" (1957) Disneyland

"How Will I Know My Love?"/"Don't Jump to Conclusions" (1958) Disneyland

"Meetin' at the Malt Shop" (1958) Disneyland

"That Crazy Place from Outer Space"/ ""Gold Doubloons and Pieces of Eight" (1958) Disneyland

"Tall Paul"/"Ma He's Making Eyes at Me" (Annette and The Afterbeats) (1959) Disneyland

"Jo-Jo the Dog Faced Boy"/"Love Me Forever" (1959) Buena Vista

"Lonely Guitar"/"Wild Willie" (1959) Buena Vista

"My Heart Became of Age"/"Especially for You" (1959) Buena Vista

"First Name Initial"/"My Heart Became of Age" (Annette and the Afterbeats) (1959) Buena Vista

"O Dio Mio"/ "It Took Dreams" (1960) Buena Vista

"Train of Love"/ "Tell Me Who's the Girl" (1960) Buena Vista

"Pineapple Princess"/ "Luau Cha Cha Cha "(1960) Buena Vista

"Talk to Me Baby"/ "I Love You Baby" (1960) Buena Vista

"Dream Boy"/ "Please, Please Signore" (1961) Buena Vista

"Indian Giver"/ "Mama, Mama Rosa" (1961) Buena Vista

"Blue Mu Mu" (Annette with The Afterbeats Plus Four)/ "Hawaiian Love Talk" (1961) Buena Vista

"Dreamin' About You" (Annette with the Vonnair Sisters)/ "Strummin' Song" (1961) Buena Vista

"Let's Get Together"/"Parent Trap" (Annette and Tommy Sands) (1961) Buena Vista

"That Crazy Place from Outer Space"/"Seven Moon" (1962) Buena Vista

"Truth About Youth"/"I Can't Do the Sum" (1962) Buena Vista

"Hukilau Song"/"My Little Grass Shack" (1962)
Buena Vista

"Mr. Piano Man"/ "He's My Ideal" (1962) Buena
Vista

"Bella Bella Florence"/ "Canzone D' Amore" (1962)
Buena Vista

"Teenage Wedding"/"Walkin' and Talkin'" (1963)
Buena Vista

"Promise Me Anything"/"Treat Him Nicely" (1963)
Buena Vista

"Merlin Jones" (Annette with The Wellingtons)/"The
Scrambled Egghead" (Annette with Tommy Kirk)
(1963) Buena Vista

"Custom City"/ "Rebel Rider" (1963) Buena Vista

"Muscle Beach Party"/"Dream About Frankie" (1964)
Buena Vista

"Bikini Beach Party"/"The Clyde" (1964) Buena Vista

"Wah Watusi"/"The Clyde" (1964) Buena Vista

"How Will I Know My Love?"/"Something Borrowed,
Something Blue" (1964) Buena Vista

"Monkey's Uncle"/ "How Will I Know My Love?"
(1965) Buena Vista

"Boy to Love"/"No One Could Be Prouder" (1965) Buena Vista

"Baby Needs Me Now"/"Moment of Silence" (1965) Epic

"No Way to Go But Up"/"Crystal Ball" (1966) Buena Vista

"What's A Girl to Do?"/"When You Get What You Want" (1967) Tower

"The Computer Wore Tennis Shoes"/"Merlin Jones" (1970) Buena Vista

"Together We Can Make A Merry Christmas"/ "The Night Before Christmas" (Annette and Frankie Avalon with The Ventures) (1981) Pacific Star

"The Promised Land"/"In Between And Out Of Love" (1983) Starview

Charted Singles

"How Will I Know My Love?" (1958) Cashbox 55

"Tall Paul" (1959) Billboard 7. Cashbox 18

"Jo-Jo the Dog Faced Boy" (1959) Billboard 73. Cashbox 59

"Lonely Guitar" (1959) Billboard 50. Cashbox 51

"My Heart Became of Age" (1959) Billboard 74.

"First Name Initial" (1959) Billboard 20. Cashbox 16.

"O Dio Mio" (1960) Billboard 10. Cashbox 13.

"Train of Love" (1960) Billboard 36. Cashbox 47.

"Pineapple Princess" (1960) Billboard 11. Cashbox 15.

"Talk to Me Baby" (1961) Billboard 92. Cashbox 98.

"Dream Boy" (1961) Billboard 87.

"Blue Mu Mu" (1961) Billboard 107.

"Dreamin' About You" (1961) Billboard 106.

"Promise Me Anything" (1963) Billboard 123.

ABOUT THE AUTHOR

Marc Shapirois the NY Times best-selling author of *We Love Jenni - An Unauthorized Biography*, *The Secret Life of EL James*, *Who is Katie Holmes?, An Unauthorized Biography*, *Legally Bieber: Justin Bieber at 18*, *J.K. Rowling: The Wizard Behind Harry Potter*, and *Justin Bieber: The Fever!* and many other best-selling celebrity biographies. He has been a freelance entertainment journalist for more than twenty-five years, covering film, television, and music for a number of national and international newspapers and magazines.

For more books by Marc Shapiro visit

https://riverdaleavebooks.com/

The Secret Life of EL James: An Unauthorized Biography
https://riverdaleavebooks.com/books/16/the-secret-life-of-el-james

We Love Jenni: The Unauthorized Biography of Jenni Rivera with Charlie Vazquez
https://riverdaleavebooks.com/books/28/we-love-jenni-an-unauthorized-biography

Who Is Katie Holmes? : An Unauthorized Biography
https://riverdaleavebooks.com/books/33/who-is-katie-holmes-an-unauthorized-biography

Legally Bieber: Justin Bieber at 18
An Unauthorized Biography
http://riverdaleavebooks.com/books/41/legally-bieber-justin-bieber-at-18